ON YOUR OWN!

How To Start Your Own CPA Firm

By Albert S. Williams, CPA

Issued by the Management of an Accounting Practice Committee

American Institute of Certified Public Accountants

Copyright © 1990 by the
American Institute of Certified Public Accountants, Inc.
1211 Avenue of the Americas, New York, N.Y. 10036-8775
    2 3 4 5 6 7 8 9 0 IPM 9 9 8 7 6 5 4 3 2 1 0

Library of Congress Cataloging-in-Publication Data

Williams, Albert S.
      On your own!: how to start your own CPA firm/Albert S.
Williams.
            p.   cm.
      Includes bibliographical references (p. 209).
      ISBN 0—87051—082—7
      1. Accounting firms—Management.   2. New business enterprises.
  I. Title.
  HF5627.W55   1990
  657'.068'4—dc20
                                                    90—36203
                                                       CIP

Dedication

This book is dedicated to my father, Sydnor A. Williams (1896-1985), who kindled my interest in business from an early age and encouraged me throughout my career.

Foreword

A book on starting your own practice—what a great idea! We are living in exciting times—in unprecedented numbers, individuals are seeking the risks and rewards of being their own bosses. This is the age of the "entrepreneurial explosion," when millions of entrepreneurs are seeking a niche and offering unlimited products and services to a rapidly changing world. Clearly, our high-quality expertise, guidance, and "TLC" (tender, loving care) will increasingly be in heavy demand as these entrepreneurial companies cope with management, growth, and profitability issues. It goes without saying that the CPA profession is undergoing a similar change.

I believe *On Your Own!* can be an invaluable guide to CPAs who are considering starting their own practices. This book certainly would have made my life easier when I ventured out on my own as a sole practitioner in a small rural community. It allows practitioners to learn from the knowledge and experience of others, which is a far preferable alternative to the trial-and-error method of the past.

On Your Own! is long overdue. It provides common sense, straightforward answers to many of the significant questions you might ask, and critical questions you might not think to ask. Yet most important, this book is not a "sales pitch" on starting your own practice. To the contrary, I am impressed with the candid manner in which Al explains the risks and hazards of starting a practice. He certainly does not represent that starting your own practice is the answer to all of your problems. Rather, he urges caution and careful consideration of many factors prior to "taking the plunge."

The book recognizes that starting a practice may not be for everyone, and that, I suggest, may be the book's greatest value. The decision to start a practice might be the most important career decision a CPA makes; this book provides an opportunity for the CPA to carefully analyze the move before committing significant time and resources.

A. Marvin Strait
Former Chairman of the AICPA Board of Directors

Preface

The information in this book is derived from more than twenty years of professional experience. Like many beginning CPAs I dreamed of starting my own practice but began my public accounting career working for other CPA firms. In 1972 I founded my first practice. Since that time I have practiced either as a partner in a local firm or as a sole practitioner.

My interest in writing this book grew from teaching the course "Starting Your Own CPA Firm," which I instituted in 1977 for the Colorado CPA Society. During the past fourteen years, I have taught the course over 100 times to approximately 3,000 accountants throughout the United States. As an instructor, I discovered that although CPAs are well prepared to practice their profession, they often lack the knowledge needed to start and successfully manage their own businesses. I began surveying the participants in my course to determine the concerns and problems that most frequently confront new practitioners. *On Your Own!* is drawn from the experience of numerous practitioners as well as from my own experience as a practitioner and practice management consultant.

My purpose in writing this book was to fill a void that I felt existed in accounting resources. When I made the decision to go solo, I learned by trial and error; there were no books to help with the transition from working for a CPA firm to being my own boss. Fortunately, I had a number of colleagues whose advice helped me through the rocky stages of starting and developing my practice. Today, sole practitioners have more information at their fingertips, but there are still few books dealing with the nuts and bolts of how to decide whether you should go out on your own and how to make the transition a success.

On Your Own! leads the beginning practitioner through each stage of the decision-making process. For those already on their own, the information provides new ideas and food for thought for handling practice development, client management, and future growth.

As I emphasize throughout this book, the key to *launching* a successful practice is planning. The key to *operating* a successful practice is client service. If you take time to make decisions about managing your business, you can sidestep costly mistakes. Going solo is one of the most challenging and most rewarding steps you can make in your accounting career, and if that is the path you want to take, I encourage you to use the book to its fullest to maximize your understanding of how to become successful.

Finally, once you commit your energies and resources to becoming a sole practitioner, I hope you pursue this dream with an energetic and assertive attitude. Although there may be times when you are disheartened, the long-term rewards and sense of accomplishment are well worth your efforts. Being a sole practitioner is exciting; once you experience it, I think you will find it is difficult to imagine there is any alternative that could be as fulfilling.

Acknowledgments

I would like to thank those who over the past fourteen years have taken my CPE course "Starting Your Own CPA Firm." The questions and comments I received from participants in this course helped to spur my interest in writing *On Your Own!* and provided the basis for its content.

I would like also to give special thanks to Terry Lee Foose, who assisted in writing and editing the text. Her experience as a business writing consultant and her excellent grasp of business issues helped to shape this book and translate complex ideas and concepts into clear and succinct prose.

My sincere appreciation is also extended to the AICPA Management of an Accounting Practice Committee, especially M. Dan Howard, CPA; Emile P. Oestriecher III, CPA; and Judith R. Trepeck, CPA; the staff support of the committee, particularly Nancy Myers, Rob Gannon, Anita Meola, and Laura Inge; as well as the Colorado Society of CPAs' CPE division, especially Gordon Scheer and Mary Medley.

I am also indebted to a number of my colleagues who provided valuable comments and suggestions. I would like to thank Terry Dodds, CPA; Charlie Larson, CPA; Joe Puleo, CPA; Charles Cook, CPA; Elizabeth Stowell Hager, CPA; and G. William Hatfield, CPA.

I am also grateful to Shelly Romig, who tirelessly and capably typed and retyped this manuscript.

Finally, this book could not have been written without the participation and support of my wife, Jane Williams, CPA. She provided the initial research for and editorial review of my CPE course, which provided background information for the writing of this book. Throughout months of compilation and writing, she provided encouragement, incisive observations, and patient assistance.

Introduction

For many certified public accountants the desire to set out and develop a practice on one's own is a tempting alternative to continuing a career with an established firm. After four or five years in a practice where duties remain fixed and opportunities for challenge and advancement appear limited, the appeal of control and recognition for one's work, increased pay, and relief from close supervision are strong motivators. But making the decision to start your own practice demands considerable forethought and planning.

During the past decade the accounting profession has changed dramatically. In the sixties and early seventies, CPAs could hang out their shingles with reasonable confidence that through persistence they would acquire the necessary clients. As a result of restrictions on advertising and marketing, the main ingredient for success was professional competence. But in 1978 accounting entered a new era. The ban on advertising for professional services was lifted. For the first time CPAs competed for clients with sophisticated marketing campaigns that included seminars, activities with media coverage, advertising, direct mail, and even direct solicitation. Because of this evolution, CPAs had to be not only competent professionals but also talented marketers and street-smart competitors.

In addition to learning and adopting innovative marketing techniques, CPAs had to deal with an unexpected deluge of information about new tax legislation and new professional standards arising in part from the rapidly developing computer technology and the increasing sophistication of business. In the past, CPAs provided traditional services such as audits, tax planning, tax return preparation, and financial statement development. Now CPAs can be expected to offer more comprehensive and complex services, often consulting on business planning, budgeting, personnel selection, and data processing.

These changes make starting a new practice more difficult, more expensive, and more hazardous. Practitioners face more professional and personal challenges than ever before.

This book addresses the major concerns and issues that arise at each step of starting a practice. I refer throughout primarily to the solo practitioner. (Approximately 95 percent of those I surveyed while teaching my CPE course, "Starting Your Own CPA Firm," stated that if they were to start a practice, they would go solo.) The book, however, speaks as well to those who want to begin a practice with two or three associates.

Part 1, "Why Start Your Own Practice?" helps you determine whether you are ready, and have the necessary skills, to venture out alone. In part 1 the reasons most often cited for going solo are discussed, a successful sole practitioner is profiled, and critical considerations for starting your own practice are defined.

Part 2, "Early Decisions," leads you through the process that precedes the actual setting up of a practice. Should you be a generalist or a specialist? What are the advantages and disadvantages of buying a practice? What is the right organization for your practice? As you resolve each question, your understanding of practice goals and needs becomes more sharply focused.

Part 3, "Setting Up a Practice," presents the three most challenging decisions you will make when you launch a new practice: financing, choosing an office location, and handling operational issues. Practitioners who start without adequate financing set themselves up to fail. Those who locate their offices in an area that is inconvenient or has poor exposure to the targeted client market impair their chances for long-term success. And when CPAs do not take time to establish appropriate operational mechanics for running a practice, they diminish their efficiency and ability to take advantage of growth.

Part 4, "Practice Development and Client Management," demonstrates how to transform a fledgling practice into a profitable, growing business. Part 4 describes the nuts and bolts of achieving and sustaining profitability: how to obtain and maintain a solid client base, handle fee negotiations, bill and collect fees, and cope with difficult client situations.

Part 5, "Anticipating the Future," addresses long-term growth opportunities and explains how you can plan for growth and nurture career and personal development. At the outset of your practice development, you are encouraged to develop a plan of action for growth, and in part 5 guidelines and a foundation for directing changes and controlling your destiny are provided—for the self-empowerment that is the reward for going solo.

The appendixes provide a useful checklist for starting your own practice, sample engagement letters, client evaluation forms, a business plan and loan proposal, and FAST-PLUS, a quick method for analyzing a potential or existing partnership. The annotated bibliography that follows describes the resources that can be used for an in-depth examination of the issues presented in this book, including one publication I highly recommend, *Management of an Accounting Practice Handbook,* a comprehensive source of information on accounting practice management.

Contents

		Page
Part I	**Why Start Your Own Practice?**	**1**
1	*Going Solo*	3
	Control	4
	Entrepreneurial Drive	4
	Prestige	4
	Lifestyle	4
	Financial Gain	5
2	*Profile of a Successful Sole Practitioner*	7
	Academic and Professional Experience	7
	Well-Defined Goals and Standards	8
	Work Skills and Habits	10
	Communication Skills	11
	Attitude and Demeanor	12
3	*Critical Considerations*	15
	Handling Hourly Requirements	15
	Anticipating Financial Needs	17
	Addressing Competition and Economic Determiners	18
	Obtaining a Client Base	18
	Shifting From Employee to Owner	20
	Gaining Family Support and Involvement	22
	Understanding Potential Stumbling Blocks	22
Part II	**Early Decisions**	**25**
4	*Generalist or Specialist?*	27
	The Changing Accounting Field	27
	Developing a Generalist Practice	28
	Advancing Your Practice With a Specialty	29
	Selecting a Specialty	30
	Defining Your Target Market	31

5 *To Buy or Not to Buy?*   33

Advantages of Buying a Practice   33
Risks in Buying a Practice   35
Finding a Practice to Buy   37
Structuring the Deal   38
Facilitating the Transition Between Seller and Buyer   40
Maintaining Objectivity   42
Acquiring a Noncertified Practice   43

6 *Which Form of Organization for Your Practice?*   45

Sole Proprietorship   45
Partnership   46
Loose Association (Office-Sharing Arrangements)   47
Professional Corporation   48

Part III *Setting Up a Practice*   **51**

7 *Financing Your Business*   53

Estimating Initial Costs and Financing Requirements   54
Borrowing Money From Conventional Sources   57
Borrowing Money From Unconventional Sources   59
Developing a Business Plan   61

8 *Choosing an Office Location*   63

Locating to Serve Your Target Market   64
Working From Your Home   65
Office Sharing   68
Renting Individual Office Space   70
Determining the Amount of Space Needed   71
Defining the Necessary Amenities   72
Determining How Much to Pay   72

9 *Operational Issues*   73

Establishing an Effective Timekeeping and
  Billing System   73
Staffing Your Practice   74
Establishing an Effective Filing System   77
Furnishing and Equipping Your Office   77
Using Technology to Your Advantage   78
Predetermining Client Policies   79
Developing Personnel Policies   80

Setting Personal Standards   80
Anticipating Quality Control Needs   82

Part IV   *Practice Development and Client Management*   **83**

10   *Obtaining Clients*   85

Attracting and Maintaining the Interest of Clients   86
   Announcing Your New Practice   86
   Seeking Referrals   88
   Converting Clients From Your Previous Firm   90
   Using Direct Marketing Techniques   90
   Leveraging Your Civic and Social Activities   94
   Maintaining Contact   95
Closing the Sale   97
   Projecting a Professional Image   97
   Face-to-Face Selling   99
Marketing a Specialty Service   100

11   *Managing Clients and Handling Fees*   103

Engagement Letters   104
Time Management   105
Fee Structure   106
Variable Billing Rates   108
Relative Value Billing   109
Contingent Fees and Commissions   110
Fixed Recurring Fees or Retainers   110
Undervaluing Services   112

12   *Billing and Collection Techniques*   115

Effective Billing Techniques   115
Service Charges, Credit Cards, and Discounts   118
When the Client Does Not Pay   118
Suing for Fees   120
Billing for Major Cost Overruns   121

13   *Difficult Clients and Client Situations*   125

Defining the Difficult or Undesirable Client   125
Overcoming Fee Resistance   127
Handling Concerns About Scope of Services   128
Managing Clients When You Make a Mistake   130
Dismissing, or ''Firing,'' Undesirable Clients   132

Part V *Anticipating the Future* **133**

14 *Planning for Growth* 135
Is Growth Right for You? 136
Quality of Growth vs. Quantity 137
Hiring Professional Staff 138
Preparing a Practice Continuation Agreement 140

15 *Nurturing Your Professional and Personal Development* 141
Professional and Technical Reading 141
Continuing Education 142
Conferences, Meetings, and Seminars 142
Professional Organizations 143
Other Forms of Professional and Personal Expression 143

Epilogue **145**
Appendix 1: Checklist for Starting Your Own Firm 147
Appendix 2: Engagement Letters 155
Appendix 3: Sample Business Plan and Loan Proposal 169
Appendix 4: FAST-PLUS Exercise 185
Appendix 5: Client Evaluation Questionnaire 191
Appendix 6: Lease Checklist 193
Appendix 7: AICPA Services for Small Firms 199
Annotated Bibliography **209**

Part I

Why Start Your Own Practice?

Chapter 1

Going Solo

The decision to start your own accounting practice can be the most important decision you will make as a CPA. The dream to have your own practice could come true and be more rewarding and fulfilling than any job you have ever had. But successfully launching a practice takes ambition, drive, perseverance, and the ability to recognize the compromises required to achieve your goal.

Over the years CPAs have often asked me, "Do you think I could start my own practice and be successful?" My response is to ask, "Why do you want to start your own practice?" Sometimes the answer is a vague "I'm unhappy with my job." A more carefully thought out reply is a firm "I want to be my own boss and have the satisfaction of knowing my work is recognized. I want to direct my own future through the decisions I make."

The reasons to step out on your own are diverse and often can be complex. There is no right answer to "Why do you want to start your own practice?" but the desire to begin a practice should be stronger than a feeling of dissatisfaction with your present job and lifestyle. You should be able to state what your reasons are and why these reasons make sense.

The five most common responses that CPAs give for wanting to start a practice, compiled from my survey of approximately 3,000 practitioners, are discussed below. Ask yourself which of these reasons apply to you. Be honest. If you do not think these reasons apply to you or you can relate to only one or two, take time to formulate your own reasons and write them down. By defining your reasons, you quickly learn whether you have what it takes to face the challenges connected with starting your own firm.

Control

The desire to control your own destiny is the leading motivating factor for starting a practice. Working long hours for others when professional and monetary recognition is limited and too frequently realized only by those in managerial positions can be frustrating and tiresome. After several years with a firm, you may want to be free of supervision. You may want to set your own standards for the hours you work, the quality of work you provide, and the type of services you offer.

Entrepreneurial Drive

Often coupled with the desire to control your own destiny is the need to satisfy a strong entrepreneurial drive. Characteristics that typify this drive are assertiveness; independence; good human relations, sales, and communication skills; and a sound business sense. If you are a CPA who possesses these traits, the opportunity to use fully all of these personal and professional skills usually makes having your own practice an attractive prospect.

Prestige

The prestige of having one's own practice is a significant factor for many CPAs who say, ''I would rather have my own small firm than be just another manager or partner at a large firm.'' Being able to hand a client a card with *your* firm's name on it instead of the name of a firm with which you are affiliated is a source of pride and satisfaction. And, of course, as a sole practitioner, you can enjoy exclusively the accolades of your clients.

Lifestyle

After the initial excitement of an accounting career wears off, most CPAs begin to think in terms of acquiring a lifestyle that balances family, personal interests, and work. Note the order I used for these three components. As we all know, the nine to five workday often extends into evening hours as well as weekends. Family and personal interests get pushed to the side whenever the firm demands your presence.

By being your own boss, you have the opportunity to facilitate the lifestyle you like. This does not mean that you will not have to put in long hours, nor does it imply that you will not have to maintain the high standards and quality required when you worked for someone else. In both cases, you will probably find you work longer hours than you did before, and your concern with quality must be even greater to attract clients. But as your own boss you have more flexibility when choosing when you work, the type of clients you seek, and the kinds of services you provide.

For CPAs who are raising families, this flexibility allows for the unexpected demands that occur when your children are sick or family activities call for your presence. And even though you must still make up the hours missed from work, the ability to make up those hours at your convenience is a priceless advantage of working solo. As one sole practitioner noted, "I work harder now that I have my own firm, but I enjoy it more and I have the type of lifestyle that I always wanted."

Financial Gain

Of course CPAs are interested in the financial gains associated with having their own business. However, it is difficult to gauge earning potential as a sole practitioner; numerous factors can affect your ability to make money. A 1989 survey conducted by the Texas Society of CPAs offers one perspective on this matter. This survey presents operating results from 3,300 sole practitioners and local firms in a twenty-six-state area.

Type/Size of Firm*	Number Surveyed	Average Net Income per Owner
Sole practitioners	1,686	$ 64,000
Small firms	394	47,000
Medium-size firms	665	81,000
Large firms	595	119,000

*Sole practitioners have an average of 3.4 total personnel; small firms are multiowner with an average of 5.1 total personnel; medium-size firms and large firms have an average of 10.1 and 31.7 personnel, respectively.

Source: *National Report—Practice Management Survey 1989.* The Texas Society of Certified Public Accountants, 1989, pp. 1 and 2.

In reviewing this survey, consider the following facts.

- Of the 1,686 sole practitioners surveyed, nearly 20 percent made less than $30,000, and another 12 percent made less than $40,000.
- Return on investment in equity is included in the net income, and the average equity was $47,000 for sole practitioners.
- Over 40 percent of the respondents are from the oil belt. Thus the results of this survey might not be representative of other areas of the country.
- Those surveyed do not include individuals in practice for less than one year.
- The profits are based on having a stable client base to serve, something the beginning practitioner does not have.

As this survey shows, the profits of the average sole practitioner do not compare with the profits of partners in medium-size to large accounting firms. Obviously, there are sole practitioners who make higher profits than those of top accountants in larger firms, but these are offset by the many sole practitioners who fall below the average income presented in this table. Being realistic about the financial gain you can realize is imperative for the CPA who plans to step out alone.

Chapter 2

Profile of a Successful Sole Practitioner

Successful sole practitioners have a great deal in common. Although their personalities and lifestyles may be distinctly different, all have developed certain skills that make them highly adept professionals. From surveying fellow CPAs, I have identified specific characteristics that are common among practitioners who have proved that going solo can be fulfilling and profitable.

As you review the lists that follow in this chapter, keep in mind that most practitioners possess some of these skills and attributes; few possess all of them. Use this information as a guideline for evaluating yourself. Defining your professional experience helps you look realistically at your own strengths and weaknesses so you can better prepare yourself for stepping out on your own. It would be wise to develop a plan of action for improving those certain habits or skills in which you are weak.

Academic and Professional Experience

Good academic training is essential for preparing a CPA to practice his or her profession. A bachelor's degree or even an advanced degree in accounting is only the first step in the education process. In addition, once the practitioner acquires the necessary technical skills, he or she must learn how to apply this knowledge. Practical, hands-on experience is critical.

In most cases, I recommend that CPAs have a minimum of five years' public accounting experience before starting a practice. Working for a good local or national firm usually provides the breadth of experience necessary for handling traditional tax and accounting procedures and offers exposure to a broad range of businesses and client needs. In addition, this experience helps prepare the CPA for practicing in the new fields that are becoming increasingly popular, such as litigation support, financial planning, and computer applications.

To evaluate your experience for going solo, look at the following list. You should have some familiarity with each item on the list and have practical experience in most of them.

- Diverse client industries

- Accountants' reports, including financial attest and nonattest and nonfinancial reports, such as litigation opinions or findings

- Varied tax situations, including all types of returns, tax planning, and tax defense

- Client contact, including procuring, meetings, estimating, problem resolution, billing, and collecting

- Professional and community contacts with clients, bankers, and attorneys, as well as civic and professional organizations

- Personnel management, including hiring, scheduling, supervising, motivating, and terminating staff

- Negotiating purchases and sales or agreements on a client's behalf (useful, but not essential)

- Specialty expertise or concentration in a specific industry (helpful, but not mandatory)

If you find your practical experience is weak, seek opportunities to improve your knowledge and skills. The more technically capable you are of handling diverse accounting demands, the more likely you are to attract a large client base. Recognize what skills need improvement, and supplement your academic and professional experience accordingly. This is essential in preparing yourself for transition into your own practice.

Well-Defined Goals and Standards

Well-defined goals and standards are an integral part of an efficient practice. Practitioners who start their practices without clearly defined goals and standards rarely get ahead because they constantly change career directions and pursue quick-and-easy schemes to success. By establishing realistic guidelines for what you want to accomplish in your practice and how you plan to do it, you avoid switching impulsively from one plan of action to the next.

To develop goals and work standards, consider carefully the following suggestions:

1. Determine the type of practice you want to create and how you want your business to grow. Target the clients you want to obtain, the professional image you want to project, and the lifestyle you hope to achieve.

2. Define your professional, financial, and personal expertise and state the reasons why you will succeed in your own business. The best way to define this is in a business plan. (See chapter 7 and appendix 3.)

3. Set minimum standards for the quality of your practice. Consider such things as mandatory engagement letters for all types of services, minimum quality control for various types of engagements, minimum documentation standards, and client investigation procedures.

4. Determine the services you feel qualified or unqualified to provide. For example, are you qualified (without extensive research) to advise, work, and compete in the following fields: Securities and Exchange Commission (SEC) audits, tax litigation, foreign taxation, computer systems, private placements, loan procurement, and personnel management? It is wiser to limit your practice to your fields of expertise than to spend an excessive amount of time researching and learning new specialties.

5. Define the type of clients you want to accept. From your past accounting experience you probably know the industries or professions you want to serve and those you want to avoid; you may even have developed a sixth sense about clients and can pinpoint those who complain about fees and bills and those who are difficult to work with for other reasons. Obviously, as a starting practitioner you cannot always pick and choose your clients. However, by defining the type of clients

you want to handle, you can work toward this goal as your practice matures.

6. Establish goals for the financial results you want to achieve. Be realistic. Close scrutiny of your business and economic needs dictates the goals you set. Just as you should not anticipate an initial $100,000 net profit, you should also be dissatisfied with nominal returns.

7. Create a fee structure for billing clients that is competitive with other local sole practitioners but also realistic in terms of what you need to meet your financial goals. The practitioner who tries to obtain clients by undervaluing the firm's services will work long hours and yet barely make ends meet. Keep in mind that your services should not be giveaways; you must charge appropriately for them.

8. Allocate time for family interests and entertainment. If necessary, set aside one night a week as a special family time. Because the new practitioner faces many demands, and clients' needs must initially come first, it is easy to let your personal life take second place. By sharing your plans, concerns, aspirations, and financial expectations with family members, adjustments and compromises that must be made can be less burdensome. Fortunately, as you establish a client base, you have more freedom for personal commitments and interests.

By following these suggestions, you should be able to develop a plan of action appropriate for you. In addition, by carefully outlining your goals and standards you complete the groundwork for the preparation of a business plan for obtaining financing.

Work Skills and Habits

In your own practice, you do not have a supervisor checking your work, and it is easy to fritter the day away in handling nonessential details or time-consuming meetings and phone calls. Establishing good work habits in your practice is as important as applying your skill and knowledge.

Always keep in mind that CPAs sell ''TnT''—Time 'n Talent. If you measure your billing at a rate of $60 an hour, and you can bill an extra ten minutes a day for one year, you will contribute $2,500 toward your bottom line. If you charge $100 an hour, you will contribute over $4,000 to the bottom line. Good work and organizational skills start with proper planning. Before beginning your practice, I recommend you decide how to handle—

- *Office policies and procedures.* Draw upon your previous accounting experience to help set policies and procedures. Define the characteristics of those accounting offices you thought operated smoothly and determine the handling of telephone calls, client meetings, filing, and general office management tasks.

- *Clerical assistance.* Your efficiency depends in part upon administrative assistance. Clerical help can free you to address client work and practice development.

- *Managing your time.* As you develop a larger client base, the demands on your time become greater. Although you strive to produce the highest quality of work possible, you must also watch how you allocate your time on client projects. Plan your daily schedule in advance, allocating time for each project. Then be sure you follow your schedule, moving to the next project after using up the appropriated time. This way you can be sure you address the needs of all of your clients.

Communication Skills

The sole practitioner should provide easy-to-understand explanations to clients' questions, have sound face-to-face selling skills, and write well. Too often I hear practitioners assert that communication is not what they are interested in, and that public accounting is a numbers game and that is where their interest lies. But accounting is *not* merely a numbers game, it is also a people game. A sole practitioner must deal with clients, bankers, attorneys, tax authorities, other CPAs, suppliers, and staff. Many CPAs have difficulty with this aspect of practice. If this is an ability you feel you need to improve, you should consider—

- *Dale Carnegie courses.* This organization offers professional, business-oriented programs designed to build confidence and sales ability.

- *Toastmasters International.* For a relatively low fee, these civic-oriented groups help build confidence in public speaking, both formal and impromptu.

- *Public speaking and writing courses.* These are offered through state societies or local colleges.

With today's aggressive and competitive advertising campaigns to sell professional services, the sole practitioner must be willing to market skills and serve clients with equal fervor. My experience with many starting practitioners indicates that CPAs typically are not good salespeople. Whether this is due to our personalities, training, or belief in the conservative, stodgy CPA stereotype, we often find it difficult to sell ourselves and our work.

To overcome blocks you might have about selling your services, I recommend that you write a sales pitch and memorize it. Describe for a potential client all of the reasons your knowledge can help him or her. For example, demonstrate how you can improve profitability through tighter internal controls, how you can minimize taxes, and how you can provide financial planning to support the growth of a business and contribute to its ultimate success. Then, try out your sales pitch on friends, preferably salespeople. Ask them to provide constructive criticism and ask you questions about your services. By role playing, you gain confidence in how you present yourself, what you need to say, and how to respond to questions.

Attitude and Demeanor

Taking communication one step further, I want to emphasize the importance of your attitude and outward demeanor. A friendly and encouraging manner can be one of your strongest communication assets. Making time to listen and showing an interest in what others say will open doors and smooth the way for easy interaction. Some clients may overlook a professional's lack of enthusiasm or accept his or her inability to be a dynamic conversationalist if good services are provided, but it stands to reason that an enthusiastic attitude and friendly demeanor will significantly enhance your ability to sell yourself and your services.

Learning to cultivate a positive attitude and a professional manner is essential for the beginning phases of your business. Most practitioners do not achieve immediate success; it requires continuous, assertive efforts. The setbacks that can plague an accounting practice in the initial stages are often discouraging and defeating. However, if you approach your work with the same tenacity and enthusiasm you use when dealing with clients, you can overcome setbacks and push ahead. A negative attitude, on the other hand, can be immobilizing. By assuming a positive approach to your work, whether you are with clients or not, and by thinking of yourself as a capable, efficient practitioner, you set the stage for success.

Chapter 3

Critical Considerations

As with any new business, a CPA practice requires a significant investment of time, money, energy, and creativity. By considering in advance many of the problems that arise with a new practice, you can establish a sound foundation for success and minimize the potential for failure.

The critical considerations that practitioners typically face are handling hourly requirements, anticipating financial needs, addressing competition and economic determiners, obtaining a client base, making the transition from prior employment to ownership, encouraging family support and involvement, and understanding potential stumbling blocks. As you contemplate each consideration I recommend you write down how you plan to address each one in light of your own particular needs and expectations.

Handling Hourly Requirements

Typically, CPAs who want to go solo have prior work experience in government, education, or the public and private accounting sectors. This past work experience is extremely beneficial in that it provides a knowledge base for making decisions and handling specific practice concerns. One of the fundamental differences, however, between being employed by others and operating your own practice is in how you allocate your time.

When you are employed by someone else, you focus on providing your services to assigned clients or specific projects or tasks; the administrative and practice development aspects of the business are handled by someone else. In your own practice, you must balance between chargeable and nonchargeable time as well as between practice and nonpractice requirements. Chargeable client work, new client development, existing client enhancement, administration, and professional and community activities are collectively your responsibility. How you handle the demands of these many facets of a practice will dictate your success and profitability.

As a framework for evaluating the type of schedule you can expect as a sole practitioner, a sample breakdown of hourly output follows.

1. *Chargeable time.* According to one accounting survey* that monitors the operating and statistical results of private CPA practices, an established sole practitioner averages around 1,400 chargeable hours a year. Realistically, the beginning sole practitioner will not achieve this, but this is a goal toward which to strive. To accrue additional income while establishing a client base and working toward the 1,400 hours a year, the practitioner can fill his potential chargeable time with contract per diem and teaching. Both options typically provide lower remuneration than normal CPA services, but they can contribute to initial practice stability.

2. *Practice development.* The second largest number of hours must be devoted to practice development. This entails lunches, entertaining, telephone calls, personal contacts, civic and social club meetings, seminars, mailings, and similar activities. The number of hours needed for this important aspect of practice growth varies for each practitioner. At a minimum, you will probably spend between four to twelve hours per week or 200 to 600 hours per year on the development of your practice.

3. *Technical update.* Keeping current on changes in the CPA profession requires a regular outlay of time. Expect to spend—

   • 40 to 60 hours a year studying topics of interest or perceived weaknesses.

   • 40 hours a year to fulfill the standard CPE requirement.

   • 150 hours a year (two to four hours a week) for technical reading.

   Altogether, you can anticipate spending between 200 to 300 hours a year on technical updating.

---

* *National Report—Practice Management Survey 1989.* The Texas Society of Certified Public Accountants, 1989, p. 14.

4. *Firm administration.*   Books, financials, billing, timekeeping, forms, programs, library update, scheduling, filing, housekeeping, and other administrative duties consume a significant amount of time requiring approximately 200 to 400 hours per year (four to eight hours per week). Since your time is better spent in higher level client work, practice development, and technical updating, it is wise to use an administrative assistant who can handle as much of this work as possible.

In addition to allocating time to handle the multiple demands and responsibilities of your practice, reserve time for holidays, vacations, sick leave, and other personal needs. Only by planning how you will balance your time to meet both your professional and personal agendas can you hope to establish an effectively operating practice.

From my own experience, I find it is helpful to keep daily time records and to schedule the entire week in advance. I summarize my weekly billable time to ensure I am close to the budgeted revenues for the given period and I schedule my personal and family commitments along with my work schedule. Although I do not always meet this schedule, it helps me be flexible without getting too far off track from the original goals and helps me plan catch-up activities in the following weeks.

Anticipating Financial Needs

Anticipating how much capital you need to get started is a critical step in successfully launching your practice. An undercapitalized venture can quickly fail. If you think about your own experience with undercapitalized clients, you can easily see the picture. Typically, the client cuts corners, undervalues services, uses unconventional financing, puts pressure on employees, and even takes on projects he or she should not, just to get the business in the door. Obviously, this can happen to you if you start your practice with inadequate financing.

If you cannot obtain the necessary finances to cover your fledgling practice, seriously consider deferring the decision to go solo until you can. (Chapter 7 discusses financing your business. If you consider financing a potential problem, you may want to review that chapter now.)

Addressing Competition and Economic Determiners

Sole practitioners face multiple competitors. These include other multisize CPA firms, and non-CPA accountants who often offer accounting services at reduced rates. In addition, in the highly complex tax field there are a multitude of enrolled agents, non-CPAs, moonlighters, banks, and national and local tax services. In unconventional services there are chartered life underwriters and financial planners in investments, consultants and sales firms in computer services, and management firms and consultants in advisory capacities. All of these companies and individuals contend for the sole practitioner's clients. Before commencing your practice, know your competition. Then pinpoint your target market for your CPA services and design a plan of action for capturing that market. (Chapters 4 and 10 describe in more detail how to define your market and how to sell your services.)

In addition to coping with competitors, the sole practitioner must also take into consideration how the economy might affect practice growth. Taking a healthy look at the past, present, and future economic prospects in the area where you plan to practice is as important as assessing your potential competitors. Obviously, if the area where you want to practice is economically depressed, you may want to choose another location where your chances of success are greater. You face enough obstacles in going solo without increasing the problems or difficulties caused by a weak economy.

Obtaining a Client Base

Establishing an initial client base will take a great deal of time and effort, and CPAs who want to start their own practices should be realistic about this important aspect of practice development. If you can count on a small nucleus of clients that assures you a specific amount of work each year, you can better estimate your financial needs and your potential profit. This nucleus of clients can come from different sources: clients for whom you provided services while moonlighting during your former employment; contacts you made socially; and in some instances, clients who switch from your former firm so you can continue to do their work.

The following questions should help you determine whether you have the potential to draw clients to your practice or whether you need to spend more time working to create this nucleus before going solo.

1. Do I know 200 to 300 people to whom I can send announcements concerning my practice and be reasonably sure they know who I am and would take note of the opening of my practice?

2. Have I been professionally active, and is my name easily recognized in my area for accounting and tax work?

3. Am I active socially? Do I participate in church or synagogue activities, neighborhood functions, civic organizations, local politics, or similar activities?

4. Do I know or have at least a passing relationship with a dozen or more attorneys, bankers, insurance agents, stockbrokers, and real estate salespeople?

5. Can I easily introduce myself to new people who could be potential clients?

If you answer yes to question 1, you can feel comfortable that you have the basis for establishing a practice. From the 200 to 300 people you contact, you should expect a few new clients. More important, this list becomes your basis for acquiring new clients or referrals for potential clients. When you couple this working list of potential clients with other practice development techniques (discussed in chapter 10), you should be able to generate the necessary client base to support your practice during its initial years.

Questions 2, 3, 4, and 5 also refer to conditions instrumental in assuring a solid client base. Although these activities do not carry the weight of the first one, they indicate your ability to "hustle" clients and should be thoughtfully addressed.

Organize a well-researched plan of action for creating a client base before starting your practice. However, as long as you are employed by someone else, be prudent about how you obtain clients for your future practice. Often I am asked what to do about clients who are ready to use your services before you are ready to start your practice. My response is simple. As long as you are employed by someone else, your obligations lie with your employer. And, regardless of your employer's response to your leaving, remain fair, ethical, and professional in your actions. Keep in mind that you want to part with your employer on good terms. This is important because your employer can be an excellent source of referrals.

One way to obtain the future clients you want while still employed elsewhere is to focus more of your energy in social, civic, and professional activities. Further, you can take advantage of your firm's professional development activities such as in-house training, seminars, and firm administration and personnel development. The training not only makes you more useful to your employer but also helps prepare you for going out on your own.

Shifting From Employee to Owner

With advance planning, the transition from working for someone to operating your own practice does not have to be a rude awakening. Practitioners who made the transition stress that two concerns should be carefully evaluated before any change is made.

First, have an understanding of what you will lose in benefits and incur in out-of-pocket costs when you start a firm. The following information illustrates what the average sole practitioner can expect in lost benefits, expenses incurred, and other costs.

Lost Benefits	
Health insurance	$1,200 to $3,600
Life insurance	— *
Workman's Compensation	— *
Disability insurance	— *
Retirement programs	— *
CPE	$ 500 to $1,000
Professional dues and licenses	$ 300 to $ 500
Expenses Incurred	
FICA (increase in self-employment rate over employee rate)	$1,000 to $2,000
Other payroll taxes, if incorporated (Unemployment taxes, additional FICA)	—
Other†	
Vacation, sick leave, holidays	—
Time for professional activities	—
Total	$3,000 to $7,100

* Most life, workman's compensation, disability, and retirement programs would range from $0 to $5,000 or more, depending on the nature of the prior employment.
† Under the "Other" category, the combination of vacation, sick leave, holidays, and professional activities can amount to as much as thirty days per year. Quantifying this amount at a rate of $20 per hour, correlating to a prior compensation of $40,000, would yield a value of $4,800. While practitioners do not take this money directly out of their pocket, they must effectively cover this "cost" by their otherwise profitable client hours.

Note that in the list of benefits and expenses, only the items common to all are quantified. Also, the social security taxes in the example are based on a cash basis profit of $20,000 to $40,000. This range is the goal of most sole practitioners, but not all will reach it.

Once you are comfortable with the financial adjustments that a transition from employee to your own practice entails, you need to address the second concern: attitude. Practitioners who have successfully gone into business on their own comment that it requires a major change in thinking to adopt the appropriate outlook or attitude for managing one's own practice. To put yourself in the correct frame of mind, carefully consider the following points.

1. Nearly everyone you now meet should be viewed as a prospective client or client source. How you present yourself and act around people becomes a selling point for your business.

2. Your work schedule requires more time and energy, not only for performing tax and accounting services, but also for developing client contacts. Social, civic, and professional activities in the evenings or on weekends are no longer optional, they are mandatory because they are an important source for new clients.

3. Involvement in various community and professional organizations, both inside and outside your practice, should be expanded. In addition, strive to increase the degree of responsibility you assume in these activities. Instead of merely belonging to a group, seek to be a leader; for example, chairperson, board member, or president.

4. The image you project should be attractive and confident. Be attentive to your demeanor, appearance, language, office atmosphere and decor, and any other facet of your life that reflects your professional stature.

5. You must think of yourself as a leader, an employer, an entrepreneur, and a salesperson. Adopt and project the image of a take-charge professional.

Gaining Family Support and Involvement

We have already considered the importance of balancing professional and personal agendas, of allocating time for your family and involving them in what you do. In some instances, CPAs involve their spouses in their practice on a day-to-day basis, and this involvement can be beneficial. However, before the decision is made to work together, you should both consider the potentially positive and negative consequences. In some cases, the spouse might better help your practice by contributing income from another job.

Regardless of the extent of the spouse's involvement in your practice, be sure you have established good communication. Once you begin your practice, you want to keep your spouse apprised of financial concerns and rewards, potential for success and failure, and significant decisions or a significant change in direction. Because a practice demands a great deal of your professional and emotional energies, sharing your hopes and fears with your family is important for maintaining healthy interactions and communication.

Understanding Potential Stumbling Blocks

Despite planning and preparation, new practices do run into problems that can ultimately cause them to fail. These stumbling blocks fall into three categories: (1) insufficient client base; (2) poor selection of a partner or other business associates; and (3) bad choice in a practice acquisition. From my experience in advising practitioners, I have found that these problems usually occur because the practitioner lacked objectivity or was overconfident.

An insufficient client base is the first and most critical stumbling block. Starting practitioners may unrealistically expect certain clients to patronize them. They assume the clients they took on through moonlighting, through anticipated references from friends and associates, and through their previous employment will follow them to their new practice. This can be an ill-fated assumption. Clients often fail to materialize as hoped or expected for a number of reasons, including the following:

- Clients established on a moonlighting basis may not want to use you in your own practice because of perceived or real fee increases.

- Friends and associates as well as referrals from these contacts may choose not to use you because they do not want you to have access to their personal affairs, for example, level of income, past business, and tax dealings.
- Former clients at your previous employment who might want to use you may feel it is prudent to wait until you are established.
- Finally, some employment or noncompete agreements require the purchase of clients leaving with a departing CPA.

If an insufficient client base exists, the practitioner can take corrective action by accelerating marketing efforts. A new marketing strategy to redirect sales efforts should be considered. Constructive input from other CPAs, bankers, and professional consultants can be helpful in defining the most cost-effective methods for reaching new clients and retaining the ones you already have.

You might consider establishing a board of directors to give you the advantage of objectivity and help you plan strategies. Your banker, qualified business associates, and other CPAs are among the possibilities for membership.

A mismatch with a partner or other business associate is the second stumbling block that diminishes the effectiveness of your practice and causes you to lose clients. Because working with others requires effective communication and the ability to compromise, it is imperative to do a thorough background investigation of potential associates. In large practices, clashing individuals can work around each other, but such polarization cannot be tolerated in small firms. Be sure you understand the personality of your associates and establish well-defined guidelines for working with each other.

Just as one can make a poor choice in a business associate, one can err in a practice acquisition. Buying a practice is not a quick and easy solution to acquiring clients. A poorly chosen acquisition can turn into a time drain and a nightmare of expenses. Most acquisitions that fail result from a mismatch of technical skills, management style, and personal characteristics. To counteract the possibility of this happening, you need to evaluate carefully any potential acquisition and weigh the pros and cons with objectivity. (Chapter 5 discusses buying a practice.)

Part II

Early Decisions

Chapter 4

Generalist or Specialist?

When practitioners ask "Should I design my practice to offer services that appeal to the general populace, or should I cater to a select group of individuals?" I tell them the answer lies in their past work experience and in their long-term goals for their career. This chapter helps you evaluate these two options. As you read, be objective about your skills, goals, and circumstances. You may find that although you want to be a specialist, it is better to begin your practice as a generalist and establish a solid client base while you obtain more specialized training. Or you may want to be a generalist but find it is better to offer a specialty and avoid competing with established general practitioners. The key to making the right choice is to weigh all components equitably and define the steps you need to take now to achieve your long-term goals.

The Changing Accounting Field

In the past, CPAs handled the majority of their clients' needs in tax, auditing, accounting, and advisory services. However, with the new age in computer information, the growing diversity of general businesses, and the complexity of tax services, it is increasingly difficult for practitioners to be all things to all clients. In particular, sole practitioners and smaller firms must scramble to provide the breadth of services that larger firms can offer. As a result, the trend is for CPAs to specialize in specific services.

This choice of action can be a wise one, particularly if it occurs *after* the practitioner has a strong client base and well-developed specialty skills. In most cases, CPAs beginning their own practice struggle to become established and cannot afford to be picky about their clients or work. For this reason, beginning practitioners usually build their practices as generalists and then specialize later.

Developing a Generalist Practice

Each practitioner should design his or her own plan of action for creating a successful generalist practice. Although you may not provide all the services your clients might need, there are ways to circumvent this problem. Remember, most clients who use sole practitioners usually require traditional services such as those involving tax returns for individual clients and periodic recurring accounting services for small commercial businesses. Therefore, a beginning sole practitioner need not feel pressured to offer more than his or her skills and circumstances allow. Guidelines for establishing a generalist practice follow.

1. Determine the conventional services you want to offer. These might include audit and review, taxes, compilations, monthly accounting tasks, and computer and management advisory services (MAS).
2. Decide which services you will not offer. Frequently, starting CPAs do not compete in complex tax services, specialized audit, SEC work, litigation, and many advisory services.
3. Develop a referral network for the services you do not offer to avoid losing clients who think you do not provide all the services they need. The optimum solution is to foster reciprocal arrangements with other practitioners so your referrals help to generate more business for yourself.
4. Consider a team approach with another practitioner through an office-sharing arrangement. This allows clients to have their service needs met within one office instead of shuttling to several locations. Convenience can be a major issue for clients with busy schedules. If you provide all of the services they need within one building, your chances of keeping them happy are greater.

Once you define the guidelines for your generalist practice, it is easier to develop a marketing strategy. A clearly defined vision of what your practice offers is instrumental to attract the "right" clients and assure the successful launch of your new venture.

Advancing Your Practice With a Specialty

As your practice matures and your clients prosper, you will begin to define special client needs. This gives you the opportunity to evaluate the type of specialty services that are in demand and to determine whether you are qualified to offer expertise in these fields. At present, a "specialist" is generally viewed as one who concentrates in a particular industry or field, such as a computer specialist or litigation-support specialist, to the exclusion of other fields or industries. But a specialist can be a generalist who also provides expert knowledge in one or two select services.

Offering a specialty in conjunction with general services is often the best way to advance your practice. You are not dependent upon one industry or specific group of clients to assure your continued success, yet you can also benefit from the lucrative returns of working in a specialized field. In addition, you can often balance the dry periods in which you do not have the work you need as a generalist.

Fields that offer good opportunities for specialities are private placements, specialized audit fields, business financing, pension plans, business transfers, computers, litigation, financial planning, and industry concentrations. If you want to develop an expertise in one or several of these fields, review your skills. Are you qualified to advise others in these fields, or do you need more training?

If you need additional training, the options include extended formal education, seminars, research and writing, and close association with someone practicing in your field of interest. One way to foster an association with another practitioner skilled in your intended specialization is to refer work to him or her and ask that you be allowed to participate in the preparation of the work.

After you obtain training, try to gain hands-on experience. Obviously, it is important that you begin slowly in practicing your newly acquired skills so as not to damage your clients' well-being. The more exposure you have to your specialty, the better prepared and qualified you will be to practice in that field. When you feel comfortable with your abilities in your specialty, offer these services to your established clients or market yourself to the industries that will most likely want your expertise.

When your specialty is refined and you establish a client base, you have the option to turn your "general" clients over to other

CPAs or to continue to work as both a generalist and a specialist. Because a specialty offers prestige, image, greater financial rewards, and fewer problems with competition, many sole practitioners feel the step from generalist to specialist is well worth the additional training and the problems associated with marketing and establishing a reputation.

Selecting a Specialty

What criteria should you use for selecting a specialty? Should you depend upon your clients to define the services you consider, or should you develop an expertise in the fields that interest you? Balancing your economic sense, available options, long-term goals, personal needs, and concerns about competition should help answer these questions in a thoughtful way.

Often your choices for a specialty relate to your work experience. For example, you might have a private industry background that qualifies you to provide expertise in a certain industry. On the other hand, you might have public accounting experience that allows you to deal with specific services, subject specialties, or in a particular industry concentration. For example, many large accounting firms specialize in banking, insurance, construction, oil and gas, hotel and hospitality, and medical and health care. It would be natural to follow through on experience and expertise gained in these fields.

Usually it is best to select a specialty or industry in which you excel or know you have the potential to excel. You should not select a specialty just because the demand exists for expertise in that field. As recommended for a generalist, I suggest you draw up a plan of action for pursuing a specialty. Ask yourself questions that help you focus: Why do I want a specialty? What ''specialized needs'' do my existing clients have that I could meet comfortably? What does my training and experience make me qualified to offer? Does my location affect the type of specialty I should offer? Is there an industry or group of industries that I want to serve?

This last question is particularly important. If you want to concentrate on just one industry, assess its economic prospects. Certain industries are cyclical and will not afford the stability you need. Obviously, you should not commit resources to any one industry unless you feel confident it has a sound future. List the industries you might offer your services to. These might include construction, manufacturing, medical practices, high-tech industries, legal firms, various service industries, hospitals, rest homes, restaurants and lounges, entertainment, auto dealerships, and real estate.

If you are not interested in offering services to specific industries, or you believe the industries in your area lack sufficient economic stability, you might want to focus on a particular subject matter or service that could be offered to several industries. Services you might choose are litigation support, fraud auditing, financial planning, specialized tax services (foreign taxation, pension and profit sharing, estate taxation), bankruptcy, computer applications and installations, and various MAS services.

Defining Your Target Market

After you select a specialty and decide how you will develop and use it, define your target market. Success in any field is largely dependent upon good market analysis and strategies. Who will your clients be? How will you sell your services to them? Whether you choose to practice as a generalist or a specialist, properly defining your market is critical.

Factors to consider in determining who your target market is and how you market your services include—

1. *Location.* Where you establish your practice can significantly influence the skills you use and the type of clients you attract. For example, if you locate in a small rural community or in a resort area with a limited number of potential clients, your target market is the entire community. Because of the restricted size of your market, you will probably maintain a generalist practice. If, on the other hand, you locate near a large medical complex, your target market might be medical practices, in which case you could offer both generalist and specialist services. (For more information concerning choosing a location, see chapter 8.)

2. *Existing businesses.* Because the businesses located near your practice tend to be your primary source of clients, evaluate who your neighbors are and what their needs might be. Then develop a marketing strategy that appeals to the interests of this sector.

3. *Personal and social contacts.* CPAs draw upon their personal and social contacts for clients and referrals. Make a list of the contacts who might be interested in your services, and pursue those individuals with marketing materials.

4. *Specialty emphasis.* If you plan to be a specialist, you already have a defined target market. However, you still need to market yourself and your services. Compile as much information as you can about the specific industry or industries you want to serve. Then, develop a plan to sell your specialized TnT (Time 'n Talent) and to penetrate the specific industry and its various support elements and organizations.

5. *Level of income.* You may also prefer to target a market within a specific level of income. You may want to concentrate, for example, on moderate level individual tax returns, income to $100,000, tax preparation fee to $1,000. To achieve this, target middle management individuals in businesses or professional organizations within your community. You can often get lists of these individuals through mailing and marketing services. In addition, it is to your benefit if you can establish connections with a real estate relocation organization that handles high-level management transfers. High-income individuals who are new to the community will probably be looking for a CPA.

After you define your target market, plan how you will sell your services. Actions you might consider are sending direct mail to homes in your surrounding zip code areas, presenting seminars with topics of interest, and distributing a monthly newsletter describing your services along with helpful tax and accounting information.

By thoroughly understanding your target market, you can tailor your practice to meet its needs. Without this information, you may still succeed, but it will take you a lot longer to achieve the recognition and success you want.

Chapter 5

To Buy or Not to Buy?

"Starting your own practice appears to be hard work. Wouldn't it be easier and financially more rewarding to buy a practice?" This question is asked frequently by practitioners who want to go solo. From my twenty-three years' experience in the public accounting field, I do not think this is a decision that can or should be made by someone else. Each CPA should evaluate this option from his or her own perspective. Without a doubt, acquiring a well-established practice can minimize the struggle to become a successful practitioner. However, as with any quick-fix solution, there are advantages and disadvantages. The ideas expressed in this chapter will help you decide if acquisition is a viable alternative to starting your own practice.

Advantages of Buying a Practice

In my course, "Starting Your Own CPA Firm," I ask participants what is their greatest concern about starting their own CPA firms. Invariably they respond: "I'm worried I won't be able to obtain clients. I'm not sure I'll know how to market myself to attract them. I don't know how to create good client rapport so that clients will come to me and stay with my practice." Because they are the substance of any CPA practice, obtaining a solid client base is the greatest concern a beginning practitioner faces. Because of this concern, buying a practice has a singular appeal. Practitioners assume that in acquiring a practice they automatically inherit a well-established business, which includes a firmly entrenched client base.

This expectation is not unreasonable, particularly if you consider the high price you must pay for a practice, typically 90 to 120 percent of gross fees, sometimes more. Although the client base may be the most alluring factor in buying a practice, the entire package must be carefully assessed. If the organization or operating characteristics of the practice were poorly managed, you may find the client base unsound and not likely to remain with you.

In considering the option to buy a practice, you need a good understanding of what you can expect to get for your money. The following are highlights of the major returns on investment.

1. *Clients.* You receive a client list and files, an introduction to the clients, the seller's right to the clients (to the extent he or she has a right), and the opportunity to serve the clients and demonstrate your skill and knowledge.

2. *Seller's good name.* The seller's recommendation of you and your work to your new clients is critical. To the degree that the seller has a good reputation, this endorsement helps assure that the established client base remains with you.

3. *Operating aspects of a practice.* You receive information on filing, billing, time systems, client histories and files, as well as contacts with bankers, local suppliers, and organizations. If you also acquire the office, you can expect contacts with personnel you may want to hire and with people within the building who can help you with the transition into your new business. In addition, you may procure the equipment and furnishings of the practice, which has the advantage of maintaining the same familiar surroundings for clients.

4. *Potential to multiply client base.* The ability to increase the size of the practice based upon the acquired client base is one of the single most important factors in buying.

In regard to the final item, consider the following example: If you acquired a practice for 100 percent of fees retained, lost 10 percent of the original base each year for the first three years, but the remaining base and new clients grew by 15 percent, what would the result be?

Original base acquired		$100,000
Less: loss first year	(10,000)	
Plus: growth first year	13,500	
Base at end of first year		103,500

Less: loss second year	(10,000)	
Plus: growth second year	15,500	
Base at end of second year		109,000
Less: loss third year	(10,000)	
Plus: growth third year	16,400	
Base at end of third year		$115,400

As you can see, the practice had a net increase of $15,400. Depending on how the acquisition was structured, the cost of the practice might have been based on the retained clients or on an amount less than the original $100,000. Because this practice was able to increase its client base and recognize greater revenues, the buyer benefited from buying the practice, even though he or she paid a high price to procure it.

Risks in Buying a Practice

Now that you understand the advantages of buying a practice, examine the risks. Because clients are the chief asset of a practice transfer, your primary concern is to maintain the original client base. Clearly, the greatest risk you face in taking on another's business is the possible loss of clients and the inability to generate growth.

How many clients should a buyer expect to lose in a practice acquisition? To begin with, most practices have a percentage of clients who are in the process of terminating their relationship. These may be clients who have moved, who are unhappy about the fees for past services, whose own businesses are failing, or who have succumbed to the aggressive marketing campaigns of other CPAs. Typically, the number of terminating clients ranges between 5 to 10 percent of a given practice. In addition to this loss, the transfer of the practice itself has an impact on the initial client base. Clients may choose to look elsewhere for their accounting and tax services.

Since the buyer wants to maximize the chances for success, he or she should understand the typical causes of client loss. Technical skills, practice management style, and personal characteristics are frequently cited as the reasons why clients choose to terminate a relationship with a particular CPA. This underscores the importance of buying a practice that is closely aligned with your own skills, style, and personality. As you review each reason, take time to analyze your own characteristics. If you then choose to buy a practice, you are better prepared to evaluate whether a given business is the right one for you.

1. Technical skills refer to your accounting, tax, and business expertise. If you spent five years in a large firm involved in management services with an emphasis on computer applications, then be sure these skills match those of the CPA whose practice you want to buy. Poorly matched technical skills can result in the loss of your client base. A tax-oriented practitioner, for example, should not buy an audit-based practice unless he or she has the knowledge to make the change to this field and the desire to specialize in this service.

2. Practice management pertains to how the CPA operates his or her practice. For example, some CPAs mail tax returns and bill clients on an open account; others want clients to come into the office to pick up their returns and to pay their bills at that time. Some CPAs are nonchalant about client documentation and engagement letters; others adhere to rigid systems of documentation and client communication. Some CPAs bill for telephone conferences; others do not. These are just a handful of the differences you can find in practice management styles. Since you need to reconcile your own practice management style when you purchase a practice, it is wise to ascertain the differences between you and your predecessor. Clients are sensitive to nuances of management style. If they expect to be billed a certain way or they enjoy a quick response to their questions, these matters can make the difference between retaining clients or losing them.

3. Personal characteristics include gender, age, race, religion, political views, dress, appearance, personal habits, and overall personality. When trying to acquire a practice, be aware of the seller's personal characteristics. Clients are often close in age and have similar interests to the CPA they use. And although there may be crossovers in gender, religion, and other preferences, each of these differences can affect clients' comfort level. The buyer does not have to be from the same mold as the seller, but if there are extreme contrasts between the two, these differences should be seriously considered.

Because technical skills, management style, and personal characteristics influence how a client evaluates you and your services, finding a practice aligned with your talents and attributes is essential to minimizing the risks.

In today's litigious public accounting environment, it is imperative that the seller warrant that there are no outstanding claims against the practice at the date of sale and that should some occur, the seller is responsible for such claims. To help protect yourself against prior claims, follow these steps in evaluating a practice.

1. Investigate the reputation, and review public records related to ethics and complaints against the CPA and the practice you are interested in acquiring.
2. Check client files and review IRS exams, billing disputes, and litigation matters.
3. If possible, contact terminated clients to ascertain reasons for termination.
4. Consider making the purchase of the practice based on retained clients rather than on a fixed price.
5. Make sure your sales contract gives you recourse in case of problems with prior work.

Ethics Interpretation 301-3 under rule 301 of the AICPA Code of Professional Conduct (effective February 28, 1990) states that a member would not be in violation of the confidential client information standard by disclosing information to a prospective purchase or merger candidate, if appropriate precautions are taken. A written confidentiality agreement would be an example of an appropriate precaution.

Finding a Practice to Buy

If after weighing the advantages and disadvantages of buying a practice you think buying is the option you are most comfortable with for going solo, then you must confront the question: Where do I find a practice to buy? Because ''good'' practices sell quickly, it is often difficult to find a practice that meets all the following needs: reasonable sale price; solid client base; and well-matched technical skills, management style, and personal characteristics of the seller. Take your time and shop around. Do not snap up the first practice that comes along. To initiate your search, use the following information to make inquiries and contacts.

1. Professional newsletters and periodicals advertise practices for sale. This is an excellent starting point. Even if you are not interested in any of the practices listed, you may be able to make contact with CPAs involved in selling their practices and learn about other available practices.

2. The Management of an Accounting Practice (MAP) committee chair in your state organization may know about practices that are for sale or that will be on the market soon. Let the chair know your interest in buying a practice, and provide the necessary details concerning the type of practice and the price range. Also, your state society of CPAs may have a practice continuation program for aiding spouses of deceased or disabled practitioners, and through this work may have information on practices that will soon be for sale.

3. Other CPAs often know about colleagues who are considering selling. Through your professional meetings, seminars, and contacts, let your CPA peers know of your interest. Frequently you can get inside tips that allow you to contact a potential seller before the practice is put on the market.

4. Local newspapers occasionally list practices that are available. Check them for possible leads.

5. Professional practice sales brokerage firms specialize in practice dispositions. These firms can be found in the business opportunities section of national periodicals such as the *Journal of Accountancy.*

CPAs often find that locating the right practice to buy is a frustrating and time-consuming process. Often, the end result is that the practitioner decides it is better to start a new practice. Although it is discouraging to reorient your thinking from buying to starting from scratch, it is wiser to make this change than it is to buy a practice that is not compatible with your needs. Objectivity is essential in making the decisions that ultimately bring you success as a sole practitioner.

Structuring the Deal

If you are fortunate to find the right practice, you must now work out how to acquire it. The deal you strike with the seller determines if the benefits and financial rewards outweigh the risks and capital investment. There are three important factors to consider.

First, what ingredients assure a successful acquisition? Typically, the most successful buy-sell arrangements are those that minimize the loss of an established client base and maximize the growth potential of the successor firm. To achieve this, the following conditions should be met.

- The practice should be stable, established, and profitable; the buyer should be financially sound and technically competent to practice his or her profession.
- Buyer and seller should be closely matched in technical skills, practice management style, and personal characteristics.
- Buyer and seller should want to make the transition as smooth as possible; the seller should be willing to participate to the extent it is necessary to effect this result.
- The sale of the practice should be viewed by both parties as a win-win situation.

Second, what should you expect to pay? Your answer to this requires careful research. Successful accounting practices are expensive. Prices, terms, and conditions vary greatly. As a general rule, the cost of a practice is between 75 and 125 percent of gross fees. Occasionally, the price may be higher. Down payments for a practice range from zero to a high of 50 percent; the norm is 10 to 20 percent. The term of payment is usually three to six years, typically correlating to a restrictive covenant by the seller. Interest may or may not be applied depending upon negotiations.

To determine whether the price of a practice is fair, investigate how other practices offering similar services are priced. Define an average, or norm, from your research that you can draw upon in evaluating practices. There may be a significant discrepancy between the price you should pay and the asking price. I have seen practices advertised at 150 percent of gross, all cash, and I have also seen practices conveyed for 50 percent, based on retention. It is to your benefit to be cautious in how you research a practice and how you negotiate its transfer.

When buying a practice be prepared to negotiate a purchase price, typically starting in the range of 100 percent of gross fees for a specified period of time; provide a down payment, the size of which will depend on the practice and seller; and negotiate a possible guarantee to the seller against erosion of the practice base.

Third, what items require special negotiation? You will have to delve into the finer details of the potential sale to answer this. Items that may require careful consideration are cash and billed receivables, typically not included in the transfer; work in process, often prorated when the work is completed; furniture, computers, and office equipment, frequently conveyed at close-to-market value; and office supplies, library, and small office equipment, often separately priced. Liabilities are typically not included in the transaction.

Valuing a practice and negotiating its sale requires thoughtful deliberation. Always keep in mind that obtaining a sound client base is the most important aspect of any practice acquisition. If you are confident you can procure this client base with your purchase, the smaller details should not become major issues. Although you should not buy a practice at a price that you think is too steep, do not haggle over small items. For example, when negotiating the hard assets of the business, such as equipment and furniture, you may want to be flexible to facilitate the sale; even if you already have equipment, you can always sell the acquired assets later.

Facilitating the Transition Between Seller and Buyer

How effectively a practice is conveyed from seller to buyer depends on a number of factors. As a buyer, you want to ensure a smooth transition; some of your concerns are outlined below.

1. Because you are buying the rights to serve the seller's clients, it should be incumbent upon the seller, usually at no cost, to introduce and endorse you to his clients. This commitment to ''sell'' you to the clients should be in writing.

2. With any transition there are certain problems or information needs that only the seller can resolve. You should ascertain, in writing, that the seller will be accessible for a certain period of time (up to three months) to help resolve practice-related issues resulting from the transition. However, it is usually in a buyer's best interest to handle all technical problems with clients alone.

3. After careful comparison of buyer's and seller's technical skills, management style, and personal characteristics, develop a written position defining how you will deal with differences that arise. Although you are doing this only for yourself, and the seller does not need to see it, it will help you decide in advance how you will solve potential problems.

4. Because the seller established certain client communication methods, determine which of these you want to continue, eliminate, change, or modify. These might include newsletters, telephone or personal visits, holiday parties, birthday cards, and seminars.

5. In reviewing changes you want to make in the practice, keep in mind you do not want to make radical moves. If a particular technique worked in the past and the clients are accustomed to it, it is probably best to leave it alone, even if it is not your style. Think in terms of making changes and modifications gradually.

6. Once the transfer is started, be sure that either the seller or you notify the clients of the change. It is best not to tell clients that a practice was "sold"; it is better to use the terms *conveyed* or *transferred*. For notifying significant clients, a personal introduction, luncheon, facility review, or walk-through are preferable and appropriate. Before any introductions take place, obtain the necessary information from the seller concerning clients' backgrounds and needs.

7. Clients in the category of "individual tax return" accounts can be notified by a letter, usually written by the seller. With large accounts, however, you should make personal contact. This will reinforce their image of you as an aggressive CPA, eager to be of service. Since you will want to establish personal contact as soon as possible with all new clients, you might offer an open house or a client seminar on a relevant tax or accounting subject. In the letter of introduction, the seller should suggest, "Please give (your name) a call and chat with (him or her). I am sure you will find (him or her) as helpful as I have tried to be. (He or she) is especially knowledgeable about taxes and accounting." In addition to this endorsement, the seller should list your qualifications and give a plausible reason why the practice was transferred to you.

8. In the initial stages of the practice transfer, do not make significant changes in fee structure, levels of service, and personnel responsibilities. Clients are alert and sensitive to such moves. If you cannot maintain the same level of service and fees for certain clients, it might be best to exclude those particular clients from the acquisition.

9. The same level of client contact or communication is essential if you are going to replace the seller in the eyes of the client. This communication process can be enhanced by newsletters, open houses, seminars, notes of interest (to specific clients), promotional lunches, and social activities. Timely service coupled with an expression of interest and concern in the client's personal, financial, and business welfare help to convince the client you are competent.

Maintaining Objectivity

How do you remain objective when the excitement of buying a practice and getting a quick start can sway your judgment? I recommend you treat the investigation of any practice you are interested in buying as if you were engaged by a client to analyze the acquisition. If you do this, you will find it is easier to curtail your feelings and desires so you can view the deal as an impartial observer might. Regardless of what the price, terms, and conditions are, the practice you want to buy should make sense to you. In other words, feel comfortable with the transfer of skills, cost, terms, and conditions. Listed below are criteria I use to evaluate the feasibility of a given practice.

- Disregard the "gross fees" concept in setting the price. Work with the "net profits" that the practice generated.
- Acquire, if possible, a three- to five-year history of operating results on a cash basis.
- Prepare a business plan and budget, including anticipated losses and gains of clients and the cost of acquiring the practice.
- Ensure that the projected position of the practice is consistent with your long-term goals, including the type of client base.
- Feel comfortable with the seller's motivation for selling, as well as the likelihood of client retention, growth potential, and transition factors.

When you are at ease with all of the above, then you can begin to get enthusiastic about buying that practice.

Acquiring a Noncertified Practice

Many practitioners assume that noncertified practices are easier to acquire. Reasons frequently given for choosing a noncertified practice include—

- It's an easy way to make the transition into public accounting for those without prior public accounting background.
- The practice usually provides a less complex type of service for clients.
- The practice is inexpensive to acquire.
- The practice serves less demanding clients.

My experience with CPAs acquiring noncertified practices does not reinforce this view. In fact, I have yet to find a situation in which a CPA bought a noncertified practice that worked well. The reasons why a noncertified practice is not an optimum choice include lack of client sophistication and knowledge of business, substandard rates, fee resistance, inadequate file history and documentation, and "warranty" difficulties.

Though noncertified practices are promoted as being less expensive than certified practices, this is often not the case. I am sure some acquisitions of noncertified practices are successful, but my counsel is to avoid this type of acquisition or, at least, be aware of the potential problems.

Chapter 6

Which Form of Organization for Your Practice?

By now you have probably decided what type of services you want to offer and whether you want to start your own firm or buy an established practice. Your next step is to organize your practice by determining what form you want it to take.

Accounting firms can be sole proprietorships, partnerships, loose associations such as an office-sharing arrangement, or professional corporations. Each of these forms of organization has advantages and disadvantages. The following discussion helps you consider the most suitable form of organization for your skills and personality.

Sole Proprietorship

For most beginning practitioners, the sole proprietorship that operates as an unincorporated business is the preferred form of organization. Its primary advantage is that the owner receives the entire net worth of the company. Additional incentives for this form of organization are the personal freedom awarded to the person who has no boss, the flexibility to change decisions at no risk to others, a greater involvement with clients in all phases of client services, a minimum amount of regulation by federal and state authorities, status and prestige, and the ability to determine the firm's growth and direction.

The sole proprietorship has its downside. Clearly, the chief disadvantage of this type of organization is that the owner is 100 percent responsible for the business. If it fails, he or she is personally liable for all debts incurred. Other disadvantages are that you may be able to provide only a limited range of services, have difficulty in blocking out vacation time, dread debilitating illnesses, experience exhausting and simultaneous demands on your time, lack time to pursue civic and professional activities and development that would promote growth of your business, and have fewer opportunities to confer with fellow practitioners.

Because the solo practitioner must wear all hats, from chief executive often down to janitor, his or her responsibilities are considerable. However, if the sole practitioner can attract a competent staff, build a quality client base, manage the practice wisely, and create a vision for the future, the profits and rewards can be significant.

Partnership

A partnership is formed by an agreement between two or more practitioners who provide funding and services to the business. This type of organization is often described as ideal for public accounting. It can be structured to simulate the corporate form, yet offer the personal service and sense of responsibility of the sole proprietorship.

The main advantage of a partnership is that it offers the strength, size, and organization that are necessary for growth. It requires minimal organizational effort and cost to establish, provides shared risks and responsibilities, permits an increased range of services and an opportunity to combine complementary skills for more efficient teamwork, and allows you more time for family and professional activities.

The foremost disadvantage of a partnership is that it carries some liability for the individual partners. Other potential concerns can include a failure to agree on a common objective, possible personality conflicts, and more rigid rules of operation.

Although a partnership is viewed as the most practical form of organization for the starting practitioner who wants to balance the demands of a new practice with other interests, it also has a reputation for a high turnover rate. Why is there such a "revolving door" of partners among CPA firms? The answer is simple. Practitioners often enter into a partnership without adequately screening their prospective colleagues. Only through careful selection procedures can you choose a partner who is compatible with your own ambitions and work style.

Typically, the most important consideration to partnership selection is the criteria you establish for making your choice. Needless to say, the wrong choice can be devastating. Reduced profits and morale combined with a loss of clients can impair and even eliminate a fledgling practice.

To avoid this potential problem, practitioners considering a partnership should carefully investigate and screen potential associates. Appendix 4 provides a questionnaire called ''FAST-PLUS.'' This instrument helps you assess whether you and your prospective partner are well-matched and compatible. If after completing the questionnaire you have any doubts about the intended partnership, I recommend you employ the loose association form of organization for a year to see how you work with your prospective partner(s); it is both less traumatic and less costly to terminate this type of organization than it is to terminate a formal partnership.

Loose Association (Office-Sharing Arrangements)

A loose association can be an attractive arrangement for the starting practitioner who does not want to be tied down to a partner but would like some of the resources and advantages afforded a larger firm. The significant advantages to this form of business organization include the following:

- Shared office, staff, and administrative expenses
- Higher profile image, due to larger size
- Coverage during absences
- Accessibility to a larger range of services
- Greater opportunities for referrals and joint engagements
- Helpful technical reviews by office mates
- Opportunity to gain insight into attributes of potential partners

Disadvantages of this arrangement include the following:

- Arrangement can be terminated at an inappropriate time
- Disputes can arise over usage priorities and allegiance of staff
- Clients may have unclear perception of the nature of the organization

- Concerns over client confidentiality standards
- Practice may suffer due to poor choice of firm or person(s) involved in the arrangement

As with a partnership, investigate the reputation, image, and qualifications of the prospective firm or practitioners you plan to associate with before making any commitments. A modest expenditure of time at the outset to examine the background of your potential office mates can help ensure a positive working situation.

Professional Corporation

Historically, accounting firms practiced under the sole proprietorship or partnership form of organization. The corporate form of business was unacceptable because it limited the accountant's liability for his professional acts. In the last ten to twenty years, there was a move toward professional corporations because of changes in tax and state laws. Although recent tax legislation negated a number of advantages of incorporation, there are still some attractive features to this form of business organization. These include the following:

- Organizational and operational benefits, specifically descriptions and delineations of authority and responsibility, and ease of transfer of ownership
- Legal advantages, including less paperwork in ownership transfer or termination, simpler buy-sell agreements, and limited liability
- Tax benefits of health insurance, life insurance, medical reimbursement, and death benefits

Disadvantages of this form of organization can include the following:

- Difficulty in having offices in several states
- Additional recordkeeping when converting to the corporate form
- Risk of IRS challenge, particularly pertaining to operating strictly as a corporation, tax treatment of receivables of predecessor entity, and stockholder-employer compensation

Although the statutes regarding professional corporations vary from state to state, the two features most common to all are the limitation of stock ownership to licensed practitioners and no limitation of the accountant's liability for professional acts. Most state statutes provide considerable limited liability for nonprofessional acts, such as travel-related accidents.

Appendix B of the AICPA Code of Professional Conduct relates to the Council resolution concerning professional corporations or associations and includes the following requirements of a professional corporation:

- All shareholders shall be persons engaged in the practice of public accounting and own their shares and equity capital in their own right.

- Disposition of shares to qualified individuals or the corporation is required when an individual ceases to be eligible to be a shareholder.

- The principal executive shall be a shareholder and a director, and to the extent possible, other directors and officers shall be CPAs.

- Practicing as a corporation shall not change any obligations with respect to the Code of Professional Conduct.

Part III

Setting Up a Practice

Chapter 7

Financing Your Business

Financing a new practice is a major step. Before you seek funding, carefully evaluate your financial requirements, research the type of practice and services you will offer, whether you want to buy a practice or start your own, and the organization you feel your business should take. In conjunction with this research, also consider your projected professional and financial goals.

Properly estimating your anticipated costs is fundamental to assuring a successful practice. Although you do not want to borrow over and beyond your needs or means, you also do not want to undercapitalize your practice. CPAs who miscalculate their financial needs often find they must hustle to obtain more clients and may have to quote substandard fees or even lower their quality to keep their practice alive. Compromising professional standards is not only frustrating for the CPA who wants to be an established and respected member of the accounting community but can also be the first step toward dissolution of the firm.

Properly estimating your financing needs is also important because of its effect on your family. If you undercapitalize your practice, you may undercapitalize your family's lifestyle. Even though the weight of the decision to go solo falls on the practitioner, family members participate in the success or failure of this venture. By correctly assessing your financing needs, you should be able to discuss with your spouse and children whether or not your new practice requires a change in expectations and the family budget.

Because CPAs are well regarded in the financial community, obtaining financing is not as difficult as it is for many who want to start a small business. Typically, if the practitioner provides a modest investment of private funds, has a good credit background, and demonstrates that he or she is experienced in the profession, capital from conventional loan sources can be obtained to launch or buy a CPA business.

This chapter discusses estimating the initial costs of a practice, borrowing money from conventional and unconventional sources, and developing a business plan for acquiring financing. If you discover you are not able to acquire the financing you need, consider postponing going solo; it is better to wait a few years than to launch a practice that founders because of inadequate capital.

Estimating Initial Costs and Financing Requirements

To estimate initial costs, begin with your two largest recurring expenditures, office rent and staff. Depending upon the type of practice you establish, office rent ranges from $300 to $1,000 a month and, in most cases, you can expect to put down the first and last month's rent and a security deposit. (Office selection issues are covered in chapter 8.) Similarly, depending upon the type of office setup you choose—office sharing, executive suites, or free-standing—your nonprofessional and part-time staff costs could also run from $300 to $1,000 a month. (Typical staff needs are covered in chapter 9.) Because your office location and your assisting staff affects the quality and number of clients you attract, these decisions require careful thought; determining costs versus returns can be tricky. Often it is helpful to get the advice of other practitioners who have established practices similar to the type you want to create in order to be able to evaluate anticipated costs.

Once you determine what the two largest recurring expenditures are, consider the standard costs associated with starting a firm. These include such items as malpractice and general liability insurance, office supplies, telephone (a minimum of two lines is recommended), licenses, automobile, stationery, and postage.

Projecting what you need to finance your receivables is the next step in estimating initial costs. In its recent *National Report Practice Management Survey—1989,* the Texas Society found that the average sole practitioner generated an annual fee volume of $166,000; receivables and work in process were 23 percent of fee volume. Thus, at any point in time these practitioners had outstanding approximately $38,000 in billed and unbilled fees. Most beginning practitioners will not generate $166,000 in fees during the first year of their practice. It is likely that they will finance $10,000 to $20,000 in receivables.

Next, assess your variable and optional costs. These encompass professional development, such as continuing education courses; publications; library services; and professional activities. These costs also include practice development expenses, such as advertising, mailing, open houses, announcements, seminars, entertainment, and civic activities.

Initial promotional costs must also be evaluated. Practice development usually demands four to twelve hours a week, or 200 to 600 hours a year. When you invest this amount of time and effort in practice development, be prepared to properly fund it. Promotional activities most commonly pursued are listed below.

	Cost per Person Low to High	
Announcements	$ .75	$ 1.25
Newsletters	.50	1.00
Open houses	3.00	10.00
Seminars	5.00	20.00

A beginning practitioner can easily incur up to $3,000 in the initial promotional effort followed by ongoing marketing costs ranging from $100 to $400 or $500 a month.

Furnishings and equipment are a onetime expense but should also be included in initial estimations of costs. Costs of furniture and equipment can vary greatly. In the recent Texas Society survey, the 1,700 sole practitioners queried had an average net book value of furniture and equipment of $14,000 for approximately three people. From my own experience, I have found the range for a beginning sole practitioner is typically between $3,000 and $12,000. I believe a budget of approximately $7,500 will handle typical furnishing and equipment needs. If you have an office-sharing arrangement or an executive suite, much of the furnishing and equipment costs are negated; you will, however, be paying a higher cost per square foot of office space to compensate for these advantages.

Also, consider the benefits previously handled by your former employer for which you must now take responsibility. These include health insurance, which typically costs between $100 and $300 a month; self-employment tax, which is approximately 5 percent more than employee social security tax; CPE courses, dues, and licenses, which can range from $800 to $1,500 per year; and other measurable benefits, such as life and disability insurance, retirement programs, child care, and education.

Finally, personal needs must also be calculated. Even though the practice might not generate the desired initial profits, funds must still be available for this critical use. The amount varies, depending on other financial resources, employed spouses, and lifestyle. For purposes of this illustration, I use a range of $24,000 to $36,000, or an average of $30,000 a year. Keep in mind, this includes applicable federal and state income taxes as well as basic (employee) social security taxes.

How much will the average practitioner need initially? Although this depends on a broad range of factors such as area of the country and office location, I offer the following guidelines:

Estimating Initial Annual Costs and Financing Requirements

	Range		Average
Recurring Expenditures			
Office rent	$ 3,000 –	$ 9,000	$ 6,000
Staff (nonprofessional and part-time)	3,000 –	7,200	5,000
Standard Costs			
Malpractice and general liability insurance, office supplies, telephone, licenses, auto, stationery, postage	4,000 –	8,000	6,000
Financing Costs			
(Assume borrowed funds of $20,000 to $30,000 at 10 percent per annum)	2,000 –	3,000	2,500
Variable and Optional Costs			
Professional development, publications, library services, professional activities	3,000 –	7,000	5,000
Promotional Costs			
Initial	1,000 –	3,000	2,000
Ongoing (included in variable costs)			

	Range	*Average*
Furnishings and Equipment	$ 3,000 – $12,000	$ 7,500
Former Employee Benefits	4,500 – 7,000	5,500
Owner's Salary	24,000 – 36,000	30,000
Total Initial Operating Costs	$47,500 – $92,200	$69,500

So you can see your initial operating costs and financing requirement can range between $47,500 and $92,200. Once you have the figures that apply to your situation, determine what amounts might be needed in your combined investment and borrowing from other sources.

First-year operating costs and financial requirement (average from previous chart)	$69,500
Less: Projected revenue	40,000
Approximate investment and borrowed funds	$29,500

Many variables can change the numbers presented above. For example, you might need more or less than $30,000 for a salary, or you might not be able to generate $40,000 in fees the first year.

As a rule, unless your situation differs substantially from the figures noted above, it takes a financial commitment of $25,000 to $30,000 to start your practice either in equity or in borrowed funds.

Refer to the sample business plan and loan proposal in appendix 3. The itemized costs and suggested amounts should help you determine your own initial expenditures.

Borrowing Money From Conventional Sources

From my experience a high proportion of practitioners borrow money to start their practices, and many of them borrow it from a bank. CPAs are fortunate because they are viewed by the business community as being honest, professional, and safe risks. Bankers recognize that there is always a demand for CPA services, and a new practice has a high probability of success, provided that the practitioner has the appropriate qualifications and experience. Because of this favorable disposition toward CPAs, most practitioners must meet only the minimum criteria for obtaining a loan. These criteria are commonly referred to as the six Cs of credit, the components of which are discussed below.

1. *Character.*   Your integrity is one of your most valuable assets. Bankers want to know you are committed to your debt obligations and will prudently manage your business assets. In evaluating your character, they look carefully at your previous history with the bank, credit references, other banking relationships, and the nature of the practice you want to establish.

2. *Capital.*   Bankers typically expect you to provide a significant investment of your own monetary resources for starting your practice. This assures them you are seriously committed to your new firm. In most cases, the amount of capital you invest in your practice affects the type and size of the loan the bank offers.

3. *Capacity.*   Your prior experience or capacity to provide professional services is a major component of your marketability and success potential. As one banker stated, "I want to make sure there is a track record. I don't want to loan money to a neophyte organization." If you can demonstrate you possess well-honed professional skills and business acumen through good references and work records, your chances are greater of acquiring the type of loan you want.

4. *Collateral.*   To protect a loan, bankers may expect collateral. Short-term loans are often secured by collateralizing receivables and personal property. Long-term loans may be secured through guarantees and certain restrictions on business operations.

5. *Circumstance.*   Bankers often consider special situations or circumstances. Examples of this include the seasonal character of a given business, its complexity and competitive position, and the nature of a product. In the case of CPAs, questions that bankers might ask are: How complex is the field in which the CPA is trying to compete? Can the market handle another professional in this field? What is the litigious attitude of people toward CPAs?

6. *Coverage.*   Practices run by sole practitioners are vulnerable because there is no one to take over in the event of disability or death. For this reason, bankers frequently cover a loan to

a sole practitioner by requiring that he participate in certain credit/life insurance programs or assignment of existing life insurance policies. They may also want coverage of potential liability exposure as well as losses from theft or embezzlement.

In addition to meeting the credit requirements outlined in the six Cs of credit, be prepared also to present to your banker a well-written business plan and loan proposal. (See appendix 3 for a sample business plan and loan proposal.) Along with the previously mentioned qualifications, by providing this material and exhibiting a confident, professional demeanor, you should be able to obtain financing from the bank and banker of your choice.

I recommend you first discuss your options with the bank you have used in the past. Keep in mind that in addition to financing, you want the bank to fulfill other professional needs. Take into consideration: Will it serve as a referral source? Is it easily accessible? Does it offer cooperative seminars? Does it have the ability to handle referral business? And, will it give advice and assist in credit card processing?

It is wise to shop around for your financing. Not all bankers are well-versed in the needs of a service business. Finding the right bank and banker with whom you can work closely during the initial stages of practice development can be instrumental in getting your practice off to a good start.

Borrowing Money From Unconventional Sources

Sometimes it is not possible to get conventional bank financing. CPAs often depend upon the equity they have accumulated in their homes, which is frequently their major asset, for acquiring a loan. If, however, practitioners live in an area that is economically depressed, the equity in their homes may have eroded, making it impossible for them to borrow against the home. Or, practitioners may live in a state where banking laws preclude second mortgages.

Where can you turn if you are denied a bank loan? First, it is important to analyze the reason a bank refuses to loan you money. Your business plan and loan proposal might not have been prepared with the necessary care and attention, leaving your banker uncertain of your ability to meet debt obligations. On the other hand, you may not be approaching the right banks; for example, suburban banks that concentrate on consumer credit might not be receptive to lending to professionals. It is wise to get as much feedback as possible from your banker. Try to ascertain the specific reasons why you are being refused a loan.

If bankers repeatedly tell you they do not want to provide financing because they view you as a high risk, it might be wise to wait several years until your financial situation is in better order. However, if you feel certain this is the right time to start your practice, you can consider unconventional financing sources. The most common nonbank arrangement is to borrow from friends and relatives. If you choose this route, keep your business dealings on a professional level. Have attorneys draw up the loan agreements. Although you may have a close relationship with the individuals from whom you are borrowing, maintain the same conscientious standards with them that you would with a bank; payments should not be late nor should special favors be requested.

Another form of unconventional financing sometimes used is credit cards. This is not recommended because of the high interest rate, the limitations imposed on the credit card, and the related inability of the card issuer to work with the practitioner in times of need. In addition, when credit cards are used, the practitioner does not report to anyone concerning the progress of his or her business. This type of check is valuable for helping the practitioner meet both professional and financial obligations.

Small Business Administration (SBA) financing is also a form of unconventional lending possible when a bank loan is not available. However, this type of loan can be very restrictive. Typically SBA loans limit the amount of money the principal can draw out and also require extensive collateralization outside the practice. Because an SBA loan is given only to those denied a bank loan, this type of financing might be indicative of a weaker financial position. If you are considering this type of financing, you should evaluate your financial position and the wisdom of going into business on your own at this time.

In addition to standard unconventional loans, there are instances in which practitioners may try the precarious existence of working the ''float'' on creditors or running an extremely tight operation. Both are risky, and the probability of failing is much greater than that of succeeding.

Finally, there are situations where previously unemployed spouses enter the work force to support the new practice. This choice should only be selected if both partners are in total agreement. There are enough pressures and tensions in starting a practice without the additional strain of a spouse's feeling resentful.

If you choose unconventional financing, I recommend you look seriously at the long-term consequences. Ask yourself: Will I have enough money to survive the months when I'm getting established and my practice is not yet profitable? Will I be able to set up the type of practice I want in order to attract the clients I need? Although unconventional financing can be more difficult to obtain and can have more restrictive terms, it can be the method necessary for starting your own business, provided you are confident this is the correct time to start and you are dedicated to undertaking the necessary research and marketing to obtain a solid client base.

Developing a Business Plan

A well-executed business plan is an important tool in obtaining funding and establishing practice goals. Whether using conventional or unconventional financing, all practitioners should develop a business plan that provides a clear strategy for day-to-day operations and defines the future potential and returns of the practice.

The components of a business plan include organizational structure, marketing, operations, and financing. Often a business plan is prepared in conjunction with a loan proposal. This combination allows bankers the opportunity to assess the practitioner's proposed business strategies in relation to monetary needs.

When you pull together information for a business plan and loan proposal, keep in mind that bankers ask the following questions: Are the objectives achievable within the stated time frame and monetary constraints? Do the future projections appear realistic? Is the marketing and sales approach viable? Include well-documented financial data, such as necessary pro forma information and projections. A banker who can easily see your projected financial needs is better able to assess your loan request.

Appendix 3 provides a hypothetical business plan and loan proposal. The content is fictitious, but the numbers are realistic for a starting practitioner.

Chapter 8

Choosing an Office Location

Selecting a location for your practice requires evaluating your client market, career goals, and personal objectives. Your location directly affects your long-term success. Weigh both professional and personal factors to establish the appropriate criteria for analyzing potential practice sites. Allow ample time for making this decision and for following through with the arrangements, because this often takes more time than anticipated.

Although the options for office location may appear limitless, as you determine your needs you narrow down your choices. The questions to ask yourself first are: What type of clients will use my services? How much competition is there at this location? Is location accessibility to clients an important factor? How much can I afford to pay for an office? How much will I need to make to handle the overhead? How do I feel about commuting? Do I need to be close to home to help out with the children or domestic duties?

By answering these questions, many of your location decisions are made. For example, if you plan to have an audit-based practice, you will probably want to locate in a downtown or urban area. On the other hand, if you have a general practice, a small town or suburban location could work as well. Once you establish the general area where you want to locate, consider the specifics.

I assume that most practitioners can assess and determine the general area or region that would best suit their needs. However, defining the optimum location within a general area is more difficult. To help facilitate this decision, this chapter focuses on how to choose a location to serve your client-market, the options for office sites, how to determine how much space you need, how to determine the type of amenities you need, and how to estimate how much to pay for the space.

As you read this chapter, you might list the advantages and disadvantages of different options according to your professional and personal needs. Remain objective as you weigh each option. Unfortunately, professional and personal objectives will not always be compatible. For instance, a personal goal might be to eliminate a long commute. This, however, might be incompatible with your professional goal of establishing an office in a location that attracts a certain type of client. Recognize that you may initially have to compromise to assure your practice is successful, but you can modify or change your decisions later.

Locating to Serve Your Target Market

Because obtaining clients is your primary objective, locate your office where it best serves your target market. Accessibility is a critical factor in maintaining and acquiring clients, particularly if you plan to offer a specialty. For example, if you provide tax and accounting services to professionals in the field of medicine, consider locating near a hospital or medical complex. Similarly, if you offer tax expertise to individuals of a specific level of income, locate near a growing residential area, determining the targeted income level by the price range of the homes.

In addition to pinpointing locations that provide maximum accessibility and exposure for your practice survey the competition. Ask yourself: Is there a niche for me, or has it been filled by other CPAs who offer similar types of services? How long will it take me to break into the business and social community of the area? Do I have contacts in the area who can refer business to me? How much promotional work is necessary to elicit an interest in my practice?

Reality and practicality should guide your decisions. You may dream of working in a particular section of town, but after surveying the area you may discover there are already a number of established CPAs cornering the market. Unless you are willing to undertake a vigorous marketing campaign to compete, you are wise to locate elsewhere. If, however, you have a specialty the established CPAs do not provide and that the market appears to need, the risk might be worth taking.

To help you evaluate the pros and cons of a location pinpointed for your target market, talk to local bankers, attorneys, and other professionals, including CPAs. Take time to do a thorough study of a desired location. It may be disappointing to look again for another site after finding what you thought was perfect for your needs, but ultimately it is easier to face the frustration and disappointment at the start than it is to recognize you made a mistake after establishing yourself at a given location.

Although your main focus is finding the best location to serve your target market, there are a number of secondary considerations that are also important. Are restaurants, banks, office supply stores, and a post office easily accessible? What is the availability of referral sources such as bankers and lawyers? Are there public transportation and parking facilities? Does the area have potential for growth?

Working From Your Home

Working from your home is a tempting alternative to renting an office, but this option should be considered only after you have addressed all of the advantages and disadvantages discussed in this section. Often, because of the type of practice or clients you want, the decision to locate outside of the home is clear. On the other hand, if those factors are not a consideration, but overhead costs are, you may find a home office is a logical choice.

In weighing the advantages and disadvantages of a home office, keep a clear mental picture of your own personality. Some people are extremely disciplined and can focus on their work, no matter what the environment; others need an imposed regimen with limited distractions in order to perform well.

Advantages that make a home office worth considering include—

1. *Monetary savings.* Most practitioners going solo want to minimize overhead. A home office reduces or eliminates the costs of rent, phone, utilities, furnishings, and equipment. Because the amount of money going out is minimized, practitioners have more money available to market their services.

2. *Practice planning.* The pressure to succeed is lessened when overhead costs are low. This gives the practitioner the chance to evaluate practice strategies and client opportunities with more care as compared to the new sole practitioner in a rented office who feels pressured to take any and all clients because of a need for income.

3. *Change of heart.* A practitioner who starts his or her own practice assumes the correct decision has been made and welcomes the challenge of being independent. However, sometimes this is not the right choice. The practitioner who establishes a home office has greater freedom to recognize his or her mistake and dissolve the practice than one who committed monetary resources to a rented office.

4. *Hourly work output.* A home office provides opportunity to work more hours. Because your office is easily accessible, you can work in the evening or on weekends. For the beginning sole practitioner this ease of access to the office is helpful during the initial stages of accumulating a client base and proving ability to do the required work accurately and on schedule.

5. *Shared family commitments.* By being at home, you can share childcare and household responsibilities. Although maintaining a well-defined work schedule is essential to productivity, having flexibility to meet family needs is often a rewarding aspect of the home office.

Along with the advantages of working at home, the practitioner faces a number of disadvantages, some of which are—

1. *Client perception.* Clients often gauge a practitioner's abilities by the image he or she projects. Office location is a key part of image. A home office may not present an image as professional or as permanent as a rented office. Clients sometimes assume your fees should be less than standard due to reduced overhead; even though you may be willing to charge lower fees initially, you can run into difficulty with your clients if you choose later to raise fees and rent an office.

2. *Zoning.* Residential areas are often zoned for residential purposes only. Establishing an office within the home can cause problems, particularly if you have a significant traffic flow of clients; neighbors might find this objectionable and report you for zoning law violation. Any practitioner who wants to establish a home office should investigate this at the outset.

3. *Accessibility to clients.* Attracting new clients to an office that is not centrally located may be difficult. Clients are more apt to enjoy an office located near restaurants, banks, and

other business amenities so that they can take care of various errands at one time. Parking might also be difficult at your residential location for nonresidents.

4. *Homeowner's insurance.* Policies typically do not cover business losses unless you have a specific rider.

5. *Opportunity for professional contacts.* A home office can be isolating. Peer and professional contacts are important sources for referrals as well as for mental stimulation; it is more difficult to make and keep these contacts in a home office. Just going out to lunch with another professional requires more time and effort.

6. *Ambiguity of time distinctions.* Business and personal time often becomes interwoven. Friends who are also clients may drop by to visit. You cannot charge them for the visiting time, you cannot afford to let them waste your work time, and you do not want to offend them by asking them to leave. Differentiating between business and personal time can be a challenge and a chore.

7. *Motivation.* The home office can offer too many distractions, particularly on days when you are not motivated. It is easy to take time for a second or third cup of coffee, pick up a messy house, or switch on the stereo. Having the rigid self-discipline to keep a schedule can be the hardest challenge of a home office professional.

8. *Travel time.* If your home location is inconvenient for clients, or you do not feel it projects the proper image, particularly if you are trying to acquire affluent clients, you will want to meet your clients at their offices. This wastes your time and increases your automobile or taxi expenses.

In reviewing these advantages and disadvantages, ask yourself: Can I afford office space? Can I devote time to my practice at home? How do I perceive the professionals I know who have home offices? If you do not consider these professionals to be as competent as those located in rented offices, you just answered the question as to whether or not to locate in your own home. Your perception of yourself is important. If you cannot respect yourself as much in a home office, because of an image problem, it is better to locate elsewhere.

Often practitioners tell me they do not want to work at home but they feel they must to save on overhead costs. Obviously, overhead costs are significantly higher in a rented location, but you can alleviate the additional expenditures if you increase your hourly rate or increase your daily chargeable time. For example, if you plan to charge $60 an hour, with 1,400 anticipated chargeable hours per year, you can increase this by just $3 to $63 an hour to cover office rent of $350 a month. Another solution is to increase your chargeable time by just sixteen minutes a day, producing approximately the same result.

For you who are comfortable with a home office, I recommend you set up your office in a professional manner. If possible, designate your office in a detached area on the ground floor. It is easier to work in an office at one end of a house than it is to work in one located between two bedrooms. Also, for clients who come to your home for your services, it is preferable to have an office that is quiet and does not appear to be used for other purposes.

Office Sharing

Practitioners who want a rented office typically find that office-sharing arrangements satisfactorily provide the desired image and professional contacts. A practitioner who locates with an established firm, for example, typically increases his or her credibility. In reviewing different options, consider locating with other professionals who can ''spread the word'' about your practice. CPAs, attorneys, financial planners, real estate brokers, and insurance agents are typical referral sources, with each offering different advantages for the practitioner.

Office sharing with other CPAs has many advantages including—

- *Shared common needs.*   If you locate with a good-sized office, you will probably have access to an accounting/tax library. In addition, because everyone within the office is involved in the same type of work, the auxiliary staff is better able to support your needs.

- *Image making.*   Associating yourself with an established firm, particularly a CPA firm, lends more credibility to your own expertise.

- *Review process.* By having immediate access to other professionals in your field, you can draw upon their expertise to evaluate and review your work.
- *Coverage.* Going on vacation, being sick, or taking time for family needs is easier because you can draw upon other professionals within the office to cover in your absence.
- *Future association potential.* If you eventually decide to form a partnership, you will know other CPAs with whom you might want to form an association.
- *Per diem engagements.* Other CPAs may direct per diem work to you. This can be especially helpful to a fledgling practice.
- *Limited referrals.* Associating with other CPAs can frequently offer leads or contacts for new clients.

Office sharing with attorneys is also a popular option. The advantages for this choice are—

- *Client referrals.* Because of the complementary nature of the work CPAs and attorneys do, cross-referrals frequently occur. Attorneys can be high-level referral sources and can help you acquire more prestigious clients.
- *Positive image.* Attorneys often offer a professional, stable image that in turn reflects upon you and your services.
- *Shared needs.* Although attorneys may not have as comprehensive a library in your field, many of the resources they rely upon are ones you can use as well. In addition, staff support will be complementary because the professional service environments are similar.

Office sharing with financial planners, real estate brokers, and insurance agents may not be as complementary in shared services, but can still offer a source of referrals. It is best not to share offices with a major client. The perception generated is that you are a part of or dominated by your client's organization and suggests that you lack commitment to your own practice. If you choose to locate with a major client, you can offset some adverse reactions by having a separate entrance or office listing.

Your office mates are a part of the image you project. If you maintain an office with someone who keeps an untidy reception area or conference room, this reflects upon you. If you share an office with someone with a negative reputation, your practice and services may be suspect. On the other hand, if you associate with other professionals who are image conscious and reputable, your image benefits.

Executive suites are another option for locating near other professionals. In this situation, you rent a private office, but share common spaces, such as the reception area and meeting rooms, with other renters. Certain personnel, usually receptionists and secretaries, are provided and shared. Although this type of office location can be expensive for the space involved, the advantages are attractive. For example, the developer of executive suites is responsible for many of the time-consuming decisions the sole practitioner must otherwise make, such as hiring and training secretarial and reception staff and janitorial service, and rental of furniture and office machines. Because there is staff to handle the needs of the professionals in the executive suites, someone is always present to take calls and relay messages.

Developers are interested in attracting professionals to their suites, and for this reason the executive suite usually features a handsomely decorated reception area, accessory conference rooms, and even a lunch room. The image pleases and reassures clients and can help to increase the practitioner's client base. However, not all office condominiums or executive suites appeal to high-income clients. If you want to attract clients who are less interested in image and more concerned with efficiency, it would be more appropriate to locate in an office with a nuts-and-bolts, work-oriented appearance.

Renting Individual Office Space

Although many starting CPAs share offices with others, and some work out of their homes, most establish their own offices. This can be more costly, depending upon footage and furnishings, but it has distinct advantages. If you lease space in an office building, you can frequently obtain additional space or move within the same building as you grow. It is also possible to lease space with options or refusal rights on adjacent space depending upon availability and demand for office footage.

If you want to establish your own office in a business complex, consider locating in a newly constructed facility so you have the opportunity to meet prospective clients as they move their businesses into the building. Make sure the building will be fully occupied and that the location is easily accessible to clients.

In looking at a potential office, always ascertain that the building has well-maintained washroom facilities; proper heating, cooling, and lighting; good janitorial services; and adequate elevators or stairways, and that entrances and hallways are well-lighted and safe even after normal working hours.

An independent, adequately staffed office projects a more stable public image. It assures new clients you are well-established and are capable of handling their service needs.

Determining the Amount of Space Needed

Once you pinpoint potential locations for your practice, determine the amount of space needed to serve your clients. This is a difficult decision because there is no way to know how many clients your practice will attract and if you will need additional space for future expansion. A move within one to two years is disruptive for your practice; however, it may have less of a negative impact if it is coupled with the announcement that you have "outgrown your facilities faster than you anticipated and are moving to new quarters to better serve your clients' needs."

If you have carefully analyzed your practice goals—in terms of services, clients, and income—you should have a clear sense of your future potential. For example, if you already have a solid client base and you anticipate eventually expanding your practice through a partnership and by offering specialized services, you will probably want to consider an office location that allows for expansion. However, if you want to remain a sole practitioner with a fixed client base, your space needs will remain fairly stable.

To help you estimate space, keep in mind that general space needs range from 300 to 350 square feet per person for most firms. One person might need 400 to 500 square feet, two can manage with 500 to 700 square feet, and three with 800 to 900 square feet, sometimes less. If you are anticipating growth, office sharing or renting an executive suite can cushion the transition. If you are uncertain about your expansion potential, you may want to consider a site that has a shorter lease life with options to renew. Even though this may be more costly than a longer lease, it gives you the chance to see how your practice diversifies and how much space you really need.

Errors made in estimating the amount of space needed for files and storage can be avoided if you plan your filing system before you start your practice. Knowing your record retention needs in advance can save you headaches later on.

Defining the Necessary Amenities

If you settle on a less expensive location that is out of the main-stream, you may find you have to drive long distances to fulfill some of your basic needs; the cost in terms of your time can quickly outweigh the savings. Consider the value to you of easy access to a post office, to mail and overnight delivery boxes, and to conveniently located restaurants. Other amenities to weigh are the provision of adequate parking facilities for clients, convenience to public transportation, handicap access to your office, recreational facilities such as a gym or athletic club for lunchtime breaks or before or after work, and access to other activities related to personal interests. Depending on the type of practice you want to establish, you may add more amenities to this list, or you may be able to do without some of the ones mentioned.

Determining How Much to Pay

Evaluating how much space you can afford is an essential step in planning. Once you have a projected income for your first year in practice, you will be able to estimate how much of that income can be allocated to office overhead. According to the Texas Society's *National Report Practice Management Survey (1989)*, office facilities (occupancy, maintenance, and depreciation) consume from 7 percent to 8 percent of the fee dollar. This is usually a little higher for the beginning practitioner, because the fee base is less than an established practitioner's. You can sometimes cut costs by taking over the lease of someone who is in a distress situation or by subletting office space from other CPAs and attorneys.

The lease checklist, reproduced from the *MAP Handbook*, section 210, (appendix 6), identifies matters to be considered when leasing an office.

Chapter 9

Operational Issues

Once you acquire financing and choose a location for your office, you are only a step away from announcing the opening of your practice. But first, you must address operational issues. By developing a plan of action for handling the internal mechanics of your business, you increase your efficiency and are better able to direct changes and take advantage of opportunities for growth.

This chapter features the operational issues that most frequently confront the beginning sole practitioner. These are establishing an effective timekeeping and billing system, staffing your practice, establishing an effective filing system, furnishing and equipping your office, using technology to your advantage, predetermining client policies, developing personnel policies, setting personal standards and goals, and anticipating quality control needs. Although this aspect of setting up your practice is not as immediate as financing or office location, its significance becomes increasingly apparent as your practice grows.

Establishing an Effective Timekeeping and Billing System

In anticipation of a healthy client base and a respectable amount of billable hours, you will need a timekeeping system that effectively handles all aspects of your hourly work. Your system should identify the preparer, the client, and the work performed, as well as adequate classification of nonchargeable activities.

You can use a broad range of systems: single sheets, showing weekly, biweekly, semimonthly, or even monthly summaries by the client; pegboard or one-write systems; time slips similar to telephone message pads; pocket calendars; and sophisticated computer software. Choose a system that is compatible with your needs.

The important components of a successful system are personal logs, a firm log, a billing mechanism, and a backup procedure.

Personal logs allow you and your staff to record activities as you complete them. They should be convenient and portable so they can be carried with you wherever you work. A good pocket-sized calendar is very effective for this purpose if used correctly. In using a personal log, keep in mind the following:

- If you do not charge the time initially, you are not likely to recover it.
- Telephone conference time can take a substantial portion of your workday. You should track and bill this time.
- Remember that the time you take to travel to and from a client's office is time you could spend on productive work. Charging the client for travel should be seriously considered.

The firm log is a central recordkeeping device that compiles time entries from all individuals on a frequent basis. A two-person practice probably does not need it, but as you grow to three or more people, a firm log becomes worthwhile. Using the accumulated data, you can check fees billed to date, review the activities of your subordinates, and monitor progress on significant projects.

The billing mechanism uses the firm log as input to generate client invoices. In a manual system this tedious procedure is executed by a staff member. Two great advantages of an automated system are speed and accuracy.

A backup procedure ensures safekeeping of these very important records for your practice. A copy of the firm log should be made monthly and stored off-site. Especially when you work with a partner or employ several staff members, a computerized timekeeping system helps you monitor staff activities and keep your profitability quota growing. Timekeeping systems on the market are designed for every recordkeeping need, and any that I describe here would be improved upon before the year is over. For the latest in spreadsheet technology, check current computer software magazines.

Staffing Your Practice

Should you hire support staff? For a starting practitioner without an appreciable client base, this is a difficult question. A secretary would undoubtedly make work easier, but the added expense may push your budget to its limit. Many practitioners feel that hiring support staff is a waste of money and that they can do the work equally well. On the other hand, a secretary or assistant increases your productivity by freeing you to perform chargeable work.

In some cases, if you choose an office-sharing arrangement or executive suite, the decision to employ others is made for you. A secretary or receptionist is provided with the office setup. However, when you have a home office or establish your own office, you must make this decision yourself by assessing the impact that performing operational details will have on your work schedule. Often practitioners are surprised to discover that small details are extremely time-consuming and distracting. To help you determine whether support staff is economically justified, I have listed the tasks typically assigned to a secretary or assistant. Based on your past accounting experience, estimate how much time you expect to spend weekly on each activity. Be objective in your assessment and be careful not to underestimate—these functions all take considerable time and effort.

- Answer telephones
- Receive clients
- File library updates
- Maintain filing system
- Handle correspondence
- Prepare time and billing
- Oversee certain aspects of marketing, including direct mail and newsletters
- Maintain the firm's books and records

From my own experience as a sole practitioner as well as helping others establish practices, I have seen how chargeable time is often lost in the nuts and bolts of running an office. Sole practitioners cannot afford to let this happen.

I recommend that you initially hire a part-time secretary or assistant, even if you do not have a sufficient client base to offset the cost. The following reasons justify this action.

1. *Image.* The image you project influences the type of clients and work you attract. Clients want to feel confident that your practice is well established. The presence of a secretary or receptionist helps promote this image.

2. *Telephone logistics.* When you do not have a secretary or receptionist, you must answer your own phone. This detracts from your professional image. It can also be an embarrassment and a detriment to business. For example, if you are on the line with one client and receive another call, you have to interrupt your conversation to take a message. When this happens, clients or potential clients are likely to feel they do not have your attention.

3. *Marketing.* Your goal as a sole practitioner is to obtain good fee-paying clients. To do this, you must market yourself and your skills. If you spend time on operational concerns, you cut short the time spent on marketing and generating new clients.

4. *Technical updating.* Staying abreast of the changes in your field demands a significant outlay of time. By leaving the operational concerns to others, you can devote the time you need to staying current. In the long run this is to your benefit, because the greater your expertise, the more likely you are to attract good clients.

5. *Chargeable time.* Most beginning practitioners have extra time for addressing operational concerns because they have not yet established a strong client base to fill their day with chargeable hours. This state of affairs is subject to change. Through your marketing efforts, your practice will grow. As it does, you want to maximize your chargeable hours by letting others handle the operational details.

If you adequately financed your practice, you will be able to afford a support staff member from the outset. Business students, retired individuals, and homemakers make excellent part-time assistants. I estimate you can hire either for 20 to 30 hours per week at a cost of approximately $500 to $800 a month, plus taxes. If you are billing at $50 to $100 an hour, it requires only ten to twenty hours of your time each month to offset this expenditure. Also, within a short time you will be able to bill out your assistant on many client matters such as bank reconciliations, data entry, listing of entities, and some types of schedule preparation for enough hours to cover costs.

Could you use your spouse as an assistant? Certainly, many such arrangements are successful although, in general, I believe that the stresses associated with starting and running your own practice tend to try even the best of marriages. When you incorporate your spouse into your work environment, those stresses can escalate because your concerns are more closely shared. However, if this option appeals to you and your spouse, weigh all factors and act accordingly.

Establishing an Effective Filing System

You will want to adopt standard filing procedures for quick retrieval and for safeguarding the records of your firm. Some firms use a combination of alphabetical and numerical filing in which correspondence is filed alphabetically and work papers and tax returns are filed numerically. This hybrid system eliminates the need for a dual search in filing or retrieving correspondence.

Most filing systems provide minimal protection against fire and theft. The use of insulated, fire-resistant, and burglar-resistant record storage equipment is strongly recommended. Guidelines to be followed in purchasing equipment are contained in the National Fire Protection Association's Standard No. 232, *Protection of Records, 1970.**

Determining the proper time periods for retaining records is a major problem for practicing CPAs. Records should be preserved for only so long as they serve a useful purpose or until all legal requirements are met. Because of variations in statutes of limitations, practitioners should consult with local counsel before establishing their policies.

Furnishing and Equipping Your Office

How your office is furnished and equipped can make a significant difference in your image and efficiency. Although this may appear to be an expense where you can economize, be aware that office furnishings, similar to office location, make a statement about your firm. Before purchasing or leasing furniture and equipment, carefully consider the type of client and practice you plan to have.

---

*Copies may be obtained from the National Fire Protection Association, 60 Batterymarch Street, Boston, MA 02110.

For furnishings I do not think it is necessary to go first class, but you do not want to appear to be a penny-pincher either. I recommend you select furniture that fits your personality and is modestly priced and that you shy away from used furniture that appears worn, gaudy, or overly dramatic. Your dollars are best spent on your personal office, reception area, and conference room, where clients will spend time. Colorful paintings and potted plants also help create a warm and inviting decor.

Your equipment needs may range from basic to high-tech. Essential items include several chairs, a desk, a desk chair, a protective floor mat, a telephone, filing cabinets, bookshelves, a computer and printer, a copy machine, and lamps. Optional equipment might be a fax machine, a binding machine, a shredder, and a refrigerator and microwave oven.

In furnishing and equipping your office, start with the necessities and build slowly—you do not have to acquire everything at the outset. Although you want your office to be functional and to appear complete, you have plenty of time to add new pieces of equipment or furniture as your practice matures.

Using Technology to Your Advantage

Technology has become an integral part of the CPA practice. Computers and word processors, sophisticated accounting and tax software, fax machines, and laser printers are commonplace in most offices. What level of technology is right for you? First, you must be honest with yourself about your comfort level with technology. Then take a serious look at where you want to be in the future.

The trend in accounting is toward increasing efficiency and sophistication in operations. Technology answers this need. Presently, modems give practitioners access to tax and accounting libraries and information as well as direct filing with the IRS. Existing software systems allow practitioners to rapidly transmit and disseminate data for returns, financial forecasts, models for mergers and acquisitions, and investment analyses. With this diversity of technological resources, CPAs have the opportunity to expand their practice capacity. Most important, they can also offer a relatively wide range of services and remain competitive with large firms.

If you do not possess skill and knowledge in computers, enroll in a computer course before starting your own practice. Self-study programs, CPE courses and seminars, adult continuing education, and hardware-provider courses are available in metropolitan areas at various prices, and rural community colleges offer computer courses nationwide. Although you may prefer to avoid high-tech accounting, you should have a working knowledge of what you need to remain competitive. Without it, you might threaten your practice growth.

Predetermining Client Policies

Establishing clear client policies keeps internal operations moving smoothly. Many fee, service, and personal conflicts with clients are the result of poorly defined guidelines. I suggest you develop a written statement or plan, detailing your client policies, which include the following issues:

1. *Determine high-risk engagements.* Depending on your training and experience, these might include certain types of audits, specific concerns in the tax field, SEC work, systems installations, or litigation. They might also include specific industries, professions, or particular types of clients.

2. *Set specific standards.* Your practice development plan and desired level of clients should work hand in hand. To enhance results, set standards for marketing, set minimum fees for different levels of work, and set requirements for advance retainers.

3. *Commit to your policies.* The purpose of setting standards at a time when there is no pressure of confrontation is to assure that you have a basis for action when you need it. Certainly, rules can be bent a little, but this should not happen on a frequent basis. Also, some policies should not be bent at all. Once you set a policy on engagement letters, representation letters, adherence to technical and ethical standards, documentation, quality control, and minimum research, remain steadfast.

Developing Personnel Policies

Why address the issue of personnel now, at the outset of your practice, when you can barely afford a part-time secretary? Consider the following:

1. Preplanning allows you to make decisions in a thoughtful and rational manner; you base your policies on the direction you want your practice to take. If you wait until your practice is running full force to establish personnel policies, you may be too busy to address concerns and conflicts between you and your employees.

2. Establishing standards for part-time and full-time staff and professional employees, including job descriptions for different positions, intended employment benefit programs, projected chargeability, holidays and vacations, sick leave, and range of hours during off-season and tax season provides structure for personnel hiring and salary negotiations.

3. Well-defined operational and administrative procedures and standards such as time records, expense account reimbursement, and new client contact reports give you guidelines to follow as a sole practitioner and later as a director of employees.

How much time does it take to establish personnel policies? It depends upon the type of practice you want to offer and your vision for future growth and development. For the sole practitioner who plans to remain on his or her own with little extra help, it may require four to eight hours of planning. For the practitioner who anticipates growing rapidly into a large firm, it may take several days. Whichever the case, take time to do it correctly. You will appreciate this planning as time passes and your practice changes or expands.

Setting Personal Standards

You are your most important client. The advice that follows is given by successful practitioners who experienced the stresses of starting their own practice and recognize the pitfall of putting clients before all else, to the exclusion of taking care of their own business matters—a common self-defeating mistake. You must take time to address your firm's affairs. Financial statements, billing, collecting, planning, budgeting, practice development, and professional growth should be an integral part of your daily schedule. It is, of course, logical to want to impress clients and prove yourself to them. But if you do not handle your own business matters with the same dedication as you do your clients' affairs, your practice suffers.

The advice that ''you are your most important client'' typically refers to practice matters, but I like to expand this axiom to include the practitioner's personal life. Having experienced the stress of starting my own practice and having counseled others on going solo, I found that too much stress, excessive hours of work, and not enough monetary and recreational rewards can quickly dampen the enthusiasm of the most ardent entrepreneur and be the precursor to burnout.

To avoid this problem, set personal priorities at the same time that you establish your client and personnel policies. Do not wait—it is too easy to push it to the background and forget about it. To formulate some standards for yourself, begin with—

- *Personal time.* Mandatory time away from the office would include at least one weekend day, preferably two, and holidays.

- *Vacation time.* Even if you cannot afford to go anywhere, establish how much time you take for vacation and, during that time, stay away from the office.

- *Family time.* Discuss with your spouse and children what they want or feel they need in terms of your time. Then, try to incorporate these needs into your daily work schedule. On some days, it requires only fifteen to twenty minutes of time to meet family members' needs.

- *Office versus home.* If possible, leave your work at the office. If you use your time efficiently during the day, you should be able to leave the office without taking work with you.

- *Priorities.* Decide what your family and work priorities are. Does your family come first? Does your work come first? Know in advance how you plan to handle conflicting family and work demands and communicate this decision to your family. If during the first two years of starting your practice you must put work first and family second, they may be able to handle it knowing that after two years you plan to reverse priorities.

Though there will be times when your practice concerns and your personal needs are put aside to meet client deadlines, by reminding yourself that "you are your most important client" you can sustain the demands of being in business on your own.

Anticipating Quality Control Needs

With few exceptions, practitioners will have a peer review requirement. It can be an on-site review, if the practice is engaged in auditing, or off-site, if services include only compilation, review, or projections.

Documenting your own quality control practices and procedures along with the adequacy of your continuing education will be as important as the internal control studies, work papers, and other documentation and procedures associated with client work.

Part IV

Practice Development and Client Management

Chapter 10

Obtaining Clients

Failing to obtain an adequate client base is the greatest fear of beginning practitioners. Generally speaking, CPAs are not comfortable or skilled in the ways of pursuing clients. In the trials of starting a new practice, this critical task can be overwhelming.

The new practitioner typically has no academic training in marketing professional services. For many, a college or graduate course in public speaking or an introduction to sales and marketing may be their only training in this field. Even those practitioners who worked for medium- or large-size public accounting firms are rarely trained in practice development. As beginning young professionals, they hone their accounting and tax skills while senior members address the marketing concerns. Only as the young accountants reach supervisory levels do firms encourage them to obtain clients on their own. Even then, instruction in marketing is usually informal and merely by example. Even individuals entering practice from the private sector are usually not well-versed in marketing skills. As a result, the beginning sole practitioner is often unprepared to face the complex reality of competing for clients in a professional world that demands sophisticated, hard-sell marketing tactics.

Combined with this absence of training in marketing, CPAs face the sobering realization that selling one's self and one's services requires good people skills. Developing an expertise in initiating contact with people and deftly leading conversations can be a challenge. CPAs are best known for their technical skills, not their savoir faire. Because of this, practice development may not come naturally and can require hard work.

Obtaining clients is a three-stage process. First, you research to define your target market and tune your practice to offer the proper mix of services needed by potential clients. (See discussions of targeting your market in chapters 4 and 8.) This chapter concentrates on the second stage—attracting and maintaining the interest of clients—and the third stage—using personal skills to close a sale by moving a person from being an interested prospect to becoming a fee-paying client.

Attracting and Maintaining the Interest of Clients

You know what type of clients you want to attract and the type of services that interest them. Now your objective is to get the word out to your target market—you want them to think of you when considering their needs for a CPA. The major ways of eliciting prospective client interest include announcing your new practice, seeking referrals, converting clients from your previous firm, using direct marketing techniques, and leveraging your civic and social activities. Then, once you attract prospects, you must focus on techniques to maintain contact with them even after they have become clients.

Announcing Your New Practice

After months of decision making, preparation, and hard work, practitioners usually feel a great sense of satisfaction when the time arrives for them to open and announce their new practice. This is a special time. Many people extend their goodwill toward you and your business because they know and appreciate how difficult it can be to go it alone; they want you to succeed, and they will give you a grace period for making mistakes while you learn the ropes.

It is extremely important to leverage this period of goodwill. One of the best ways to take advantage of it is to get your name in front of as many people as possible. You can do this initially by sending announcements to prospective clients and client sources describing your new practice and its services. From the responses you receive, you should develop an initial client nucleus and referral base from which to build your practice.

Keep the design of your announcement simple and modest. Neatly hand-addressed envelopes with a distinctive stamp are preferable to labels and postage meters. The announcement should inform the recipient of the opening of the practice and the general services offered. Specific details of services can be conveyed in later communications.

From the AICPA's viewpoint, you can send announcements to whomever you wish; there are no restrictions. However, some state boards of accountancy might have constraints, so it would be wise to review local accounting ethics standards. There are two types of people to include on your announcement list: those who might use your services, and those who might refer clients to you. Following are some specific suggestions for your announcement list.

1. *Professional associates.* Send announcements to all the CPAs you know. Your professional peers can be good referral sources and may have helpful tips for establishing a client base.

2. *Potential referral sources.* Attorneys, bankers, brokers, and other professionals are excellent referral sources. Often the work you do complements their work and can create a mutually satisfactory exchange of services. Their names and addresses can be found in professional association directories.

3. *Contacts from civic and social activities.* Contacts you make at civic and social functions can be prospective clients. Although people may be gathering together for the purpose of socializing, business is always a secondary possibility. You can obtain names and addresses by using membership rosters from civic or social groups you attend.

4. *Friends.* Many of your friends may already have a CPA they use and like. Obviously, you do not want to put pressure on them to switch to you. However, your friends may be excellent referral sources. Let them know the type of work you do and the type of client you seek.

5. *Family members.* You may receive business from family members. However, it is probably best to use family members primarily as referral sources and avoid accepting them as clients. Because of the dynamics of family relationships, practitioners sometimes find that relatives expect them to provide services for reduced rates or no rates at all. When trying to establish a fledgling practice, you can do without having your time and energy taken up by low-paying or non-paying family clients.

6. *Previous clients.* Former clients may want to continue working with you even though this may mean disassociating themselves from the firm you were once with. Although you do not want to alienate your previous employer, the client is the one who ultimately must choose whom he or she wants to employ for accounting and tax services. Because some state boards of accountancy are more restrictive regarding direct, uninvited solicitation than is the AICPA, be sure to consider your own locale's professional environment and rules. Also, if you were subject to an employment agreement or restrictive covenant at your former employer, you need to consider the ramifications of a potential violation.

If the size of your office supports it, you might include an invitation to an open house celebrating your new practice. Many people, particularly those you invite in person or by telephone, will use the opportunity to take an hour or two off, preferably in late afternoon, to wish you well. Having a good turnout for your open house reinforces the image that you are destined for success.

After your announcements go out, you will get a response in the form of potential clients as well as good wishes. At this point, follow-up is extremely important. Call key potential clients or referral sources a few weeks after sending your announcement. Bring the conversation quickly to your practice. Let the person know it is off to a good start, and when the opportunity arises, ask whether there is some way you can be of service or, if appropriate, suggest you meet to discuss working together. By being aggressive, to this degree, you impress potential clients with your determination to secure the type of business you want.

Seeking Referrals

Traditionally, CPAs marketed their services passively, mainly relying on a network of acquaintances to provide them with referrals. Today, referrals are still an important aspect of client development, but because of the aggressive marketing methods now permitted in the accounting profession, competition is fiercer. CPAs must actively seek and maintain their referral sources to survive. With the changes in marketing techniques, the accounting profession is taking a broader look at its definition of referral sources.

For the practitioner who is about to go solo, it is important to understand the dynamics surrounding referrals. Be aware that your competition is aggressive in supporting its referral sources. AICPA ethics standards that are under consideration may in the near future allow all CPAs to pay referral fees for clients under certain conditions.* Many large firms hire staff or assign partners to focus on marketing, which means giving a substantial amount of attention to referral services. Other firms use marketing consultants.

To foster a steady flow of referrals, keep track of which sources are productive, marginal, or nonproductive in generating clients. Maintain regular contact with productive and marginal sources, and deemphasize the nonproductive sources. Whenever you get a new client, promptly acknowledge the referral source with a phone call or letter. Having lunch or dinner on a regular basis with productive sources is an effective and inexpensive means of facilitating new client contacts. Remember, you want your referral sources to feel appreciated. Whatever the means of acknowledgment you use, your message should be, I appreciate the confidence you continue to show in me.

Your most valuable source of referrals is your existing client base. The key to generating goodwill and referrals from this source is to provide the best service possible for reasonable and competitive fees. Make sure you complete projects on time, according to the agreed-upon arrangements. As you develop a good rapport with clients, be explicit in letting them know that you would appreciate their referring more business to you.

The next most significant source of referrals is other professionals—attorneys, bankers, brokers, and CPAs. A relationship with a colleague who serves as a referral source can be more valuable than any one client. Even though you may be faced with the pressure of meeting the demands of fee-paying clients, always allocate time to nurture these relationships; they may be your future. Reciprocity in these relationships comes from cross-referrals, using the services of your sources, and networking. Be sure to keep the quality of the professionals in your referral network high, because the recommendations you give clients reflect on you.

---

*Agreement containing consent order to Cease and Desist (File No. 851 0020), in the matter of the American Institute of Certified Public Accountants, a corporation, before the Federal Trade Commission.

Finally, do not overlook other CPAs as referral sources. With the increasing specialization and complexities in the profession, you and your fellow CPAs can candidly explore ways to share clients among yourselves.

Converting Clients From Your Previous Firm

The issue of converting clients from a previous employer frequently arises in group study seminars I teach. There are, of course, varying ethical constraints imposed by state boards of accountancy and local professional societies. Check these before making your transition so that you know what is considered fair professional conduct as concerns client conversions. Of significance are the restrictions imposed by any employment agreement you may have with your previous employer. These agreements can be difficult to enforce. However, they can result in litigation which, with the cost and negative publicity, can hamper a new practitioner.

Clients want to work with the CPA or firm with which they feel most comfortable. The decision to follow you to your new practice or remain with the accounting firm that employed you is usually clear; it was made during the months or years of service the client already received. So in reality, overt actions by either you or your previous employer have little effect on the client. It is likely that if you and your previous firm each claim a client as your own, the client may drop you both.

The major focus should not be on converting clients but on leaving your previous employer amicably. Most employers expect to lose some business in such transitions and, so long as you are not overly aggressive, you can probably maintain good relations. By maintaining a good rapport, you leave the door open for referrals, overflow work, backup and review, and joint engagements.

Using Direct Marketing Techniques

Direct marketing techniques help you reach people not normally contacted through your referral network. By using this method of "selling," you extend your pool of potential clients beyond your sphere of personal influence. In general, direct marketing leads require more effort than referrals because the people you approach know less about you. Options include advertising, direct mail campaigns, telephone soliciting, writing articles for local newspapers, and giving seminars.

Advertising. Advertising your practice and services can bring profitable returns. Some forms of media advertising to consider include—

- *Yellow pages.* Advertising in the Yellow Pages can be an effective method for circulating word of your services. Talk to fellow practitioners who advertise in the Yellow Pages to learn their results. Also, recognize that potential clients who contact you as a result of Yellow Page advertising are often most concerned with location or price. Conducting a thorough client interview before taking work from these potential clients is to your advantage to avoid possible undesirable clients.

- *Newspapers or local publications.* I have found that advertising in local newspapers and publications is usually less successful than Yellow Page ads. The fact that CPAs have not experimented with it extensively is a probable indication of a lack of results. It does seem to work for some who advertise specific services such as tax preparation and financial planning. Being selective about placement, such as the business section or personal services directory in the classified section, would be wise.

- *Radio and TV.* Radio and television are used sparingly by most CPAs because often the returns are low and the cost high. Unless you enjoy new conquests, and have the funds for it, I suggest not using this form of advertising until it becomes more widely recognized and accepted. The practitioners I know who appear on local cable television talk shows and advertise on the radio have not had overwhelming results.

- *Miscellaneous advertising.* Miscellaneous forms of advertising can be fun and profitable. For example, I have seen advertisements on bulletin boards at local grocery stores, lapel buttons that state, "Have you hugged your CPA today?," and T-shirts and bumper stickers that provide CPA telephone numbers and service information. In addition, I know CPAs who advertise their services through Welcome Wagon programs, through athletic activity sponsorship, on city maps distributed by the local chamber of commerce, and by giving free consultation or service as prizes on educational television fund-raising projects.

Within the parameters of your own state's restrictions on how and where you advertise and market your services, experiment with different methods until you find the ones that are most cost effective and provide the greatest new client contacts. Consider those discussed below.

Direct Mail. Direct mail campaigns for CPAs get mixed reviews. Success in direct mail is often claimed when response is only one or 2 percent. Many factors affect it, such as quality of the materials sent, quality of the mailing list, and follow-up procedures. If you choose this method, look carefully at its cost effectiveness. I suggest talking to other professionals in the area who tried direct mail or professional direct mail services. Typical types of mail lists include new homeowners, new businesses, homeowners' associations, attorneys, bankers, or specific types of businesses.

Telephone Solicitation. Telephone solicitation or cold calling is not a common marketing technique for CPAs. This technique is increasing in some cities. As with direct mail, I suggest you ask other professionals about their experiences with phone solicitation. Cold calling is hard work and requires special skills to be successful. If you want to use this form of marketing, I recommend that you investigate marketing firms that train you in effective calling techniques before investing a large amount of personal or staff time. If you decide to use this method, it can be applied to your target market, such as homeowners or industries.

Articles in Local Publications. Periodic articles in local publications such as newspapers or business publications can produce clients over the short term. But more important, articles promote name recognition, and this might pay off over a span of several years. You can write original pieces for publications or buy space and reprint "tax tip" articles purchased from industry sources. Following are some helpful guidelines.

1. Keep the article easy to understand—use language that is simple and to the point; especially avoid technical jargon.
2. Select publications read by your target market.
3. Choose topics of concern to the reader audience, topics that have timely interest and are keyed to economic events or legislative changes.

4. Avoid giving answers that are too simplistic to complex issues. It is important to emphasize the needs of each specific situation; otherwise, you may inadvertently set a client's expectations for a simple answer that will not work in his case.

5. Make sure you get credit. Your name and business affiliation should appear as a byline, next to your picture. Whenever possible, end your article with an invitation for readers to call if they have questions.

Seminars. The half-day or evening seminar is an effective method for demonstrating your expertise in special fields. Seminars require a great deal of work. To be successful, you must do a good job publicizing the event, delivering the material, and following up the leads generated. Once you develop a seminar program, repeat it as often as possible to make it cost and time effective. If the topic aims at the general public, you can deliver your seminar through various organizations such as the chamber of commerce, civic groups, industry trade groups, and even commercial organizations such as banks. Guidelines for giving seminars follow.

1. Know your topic and presentation thoroughly. Comprehensive research and rehearsing your presentation come through loud and clear to your audience. Never bluff; pretending you know something you do not can be embarrassing and professionally damaging.

2. Keep the presentation straightforward. Do not "talk technical" with lay people. They might be impressed with your knowledge but could assume that they cannot communicate with you.

3. Use visual aids. Viewgraphs for an overhead projector help guide the talk and make points. Use graphs and charts where appropriate, and try to include some humor, perhaps in the form of a cartoon.

4. Provide a handout. The handout should contain your name, address, phone number, seminar outline, and copies of the key visual aids that restate the message.

5. Do not let tough questions faze you. Respond to difficult questions in one-on-one discussions during breaks; do not slow down the seminar. If you need clarification, take notes on the questions and answer them with follow-up phone calls.

6. Collect names, addresses, and phone numbers of all attendees. They expressed an interest by attending; this information allows you to follow up. Make notes opposite names on a copy of the attendance list to help with follow up.

7. Follow up. After all your efforts in organizing the seminar, make sure you call or write attendees to thank them for their participation. If appropriate, expand or clarify questions they have. Invite them to call for more help. Add the attendees to your next list for direct mail or newsletters.

Leveraging Your Civic and Social Activities

When you are in practice for yourself, treat everyone you meet as a potential client. By learning to take the initiative, you can generate new business out of your civic and social activities. This aggressive attitude is not only acceptable, it is now prevalent in the profession.

Obviously, you should not look on every social or civic engagement as a mercenary opportunity to close business. But by being aware of people and expressing an interest in them, you have the chance to open dialogue that would lead to a new client. It is easy to forget what to say in a situation where you are trying to impress someone, so do not overdo it. The following are a few pointers I use in these situations.

1. Begin the conversation with a firm handshake, a warm greeting, and an introduction of yourself.

2. Get the other person to talk about himself or herself, why he or she is at this function, what line of work he or she is in. Follow up with questions that show interest, such as, ''How did you get into that line of work?'' or ''Have you always been in that field?''

3. Lead the conversation, if appropriate, toward taxes, the economy, business, or government regulation. You can then, unobtrusively, show your knowledge.

4. If you are trying to meet a specific person, do some advance research. The extra information helps you with the conversation.

5. Keep abreast of business issues in the press. The better read you are, the better able you will be to make intelligent statements or respond to questions.

Civic and professional activities offer a chance to contribute to your community and give you an opportunity to meet potential clients. However, make sure you enjoy the activity for its own merits. Organizations or activities entered solely to gain clients will usually not be rewarding.

Aspire to a leadership position. Start as an active member, move to a committee chair position, next to the board of directors and, if possible, the presidency. As you rise in the organization you have the opportunity to demonstrate your business acumen. If you consider accepting the treasurer's position in an organization, make sure it is a high-profile position.

A speaker's bureau can provide good exposure. Speakers are an important aspect of the organization's image with the general public. Your active participation in it or role as chair can put you in front of many people.

Maintaining Contact

As you establish a client base and a list of potential clients for your new practice, you need to tune your marketing efforts to allocate time and energy to maintaining that base. Your objectives in maintaining contact are to show your ongoing interest, remind your clients of ways your services can help them, and prevent them from yielding to the marketing pressures of other CPAs. Let us examine the chief ways of staying in touch.

Newsletters. Newsletters are an excellent way to maintain contact with existing clients, referral sources, and potential clients. They are also a good follow-up vehicle after an initial client contact; they reflect a commitment to the communication process. In addition, because newsletter programs can be handled by a secretary, they are an easy method for maintaining contact without causing the practitioner to take time away from client work. Practitioners can write their own newsletters, but it is time consuming and expensive. An easier option is to purchase newsletters written for distribution by CPAs. The most common are *The Client Monthly Alert,* published by the editors of the *Practical Accountant* (a Warren, Gorham & Lamont publication), and the *Client Bulletin* from the AICPA. You can acquire these at modest cost with or without your name imprinted. Another option is to obtain rights to reprint and distribute a commercial newsletter in your area. I have successfully used Mostad and Christenson's newsletter *The Financial Alert*.

Personal Notes. A short follow-up letter on a topic of interest or a copy of an article with a note from you are effective ways of extending your personal interest. They show that you are thinking about the recipient. This approach obviously takes more of your time than bulk mailing a newsletter, so you must select your targets judiciously.

Periodic Phone Calls. Phone calls have the distinct advantage of giving you an immediate reading on the reactions of a client or potential client. The reasons most commonly cited by clients for changing accountants are inadequate service, untimely service, lack of personal contact, and change in personnel. With a phone call you can read signs of these concerns and address them immediately.

Business Meals and Personal Meetings. Important clients, referral sources, or potential clients need the time and attention of personal meetings. A business meal is an excellent way to share time. You can have an early breakfast, a lunch, or an evening get-together. If you meet and dine with potential clients, the cost of this meal falls on you. When you are in the process of obtaining a new client, "Let's go Dutch," or "You get it this time, I'll get it next," is not appropriate. After obtaining the client, picking up the tab becomes more flexible. In addition to business meals, other activities such as sporting or cultural events, social gatherings, and seminars given by other professionals offer enjoyable opportunities for socializing and spending time with clients. When it is appropriate, the topic of the meeting can be business, but do not undervalue the importance of just spending time with your clients to get to know them.

   As a final comment, let me emphasize the importance of maintaining your contact list. It is easy to be careless about updating your list with a new address or phone number. Do not procrastinate, do it as soon as you receive new information. Give some thought, also, on how you physically maintain your lists—a card file, an address book, or a computer system. Make the system easy to use, and allow space for keeping brief notes on the client. Periodically make a backup of the list to store in a safe, off-site location.

Closing the Sale

The marketing tools just discussed get people in the door. To be successful with your new practice, however, you must use both your professional and personal skills to transform interested contacts into loyal clients. The major abilities needed to accomplish this transaction are projecting a professional image and making face-to-face sales.

Projecting a Professional Image

Books have been written about the importance of the first five minutes of a business engagement. Clients are won and major deals struck based on the impressions made during these critical introductory moments. Accountants with a proven success record in acquiring new clients emphasize the importance of projecting a professional image of competence, reliability, and honesty during the first five minutes and systematically reinforcing this image with every subsequent opportunity.

A "selling" professional image depends on an attractive personal presentation and environment. The components of a selling image are—

- *Dress.* Clean, neat, and conservative are the basic guidelines for CPAs. Successful salespeople of sophisticated products recommend that you purchase good-looking natural-fiber clothing. Quality dressing helps attract quality clients. Men should choose wool suits, cotton shirts, and silk ties. Women have greater options in style and fabric choices, but whatever they choose should reflect a professional, no-nonsense image. If you need guidance upgrading your wardrobe, work with a salesperson at a high-quality clothing store.

- *Physical presence.* Posture, firmness of handshake, and voice are aspects of demeanor that are critical to making a good impression. They are the first indicators of your professional and personal skills. If you are not comfortable with how you present yourself, ask others to help you role play to develop the style you want. You can also seek help from professionals in public speaking and presentation.

- *Speech and expressions.* Correct grammar, good vocabulary, appropriate use of words and expressions, good pronunciation, and projection are essential. Remember, you must first sell yourself to a potential client before you can settle down to do the technical work you enjoy. An articulate presentation of who you are and what you have to offer can be vital to acquiring new clients. Again, if you are not comfortable, practice what you want to say in front of a mirror or with friends until you are confident.

- *Concern.*   You should show clients that you are interested in their individual problems and do not think of them as merely money in the bank. Keep track of personal information about your clients, such as the names of spouses and children and their particular interests.

- *Office appearance.*   Your work environment makes a dramatic statement about your personal and professional habits. A clean, neat, and well-organized office assures clients you are professional and run a "tight ship." A well-decorated office takes this statement one step further. When clients feel at home in an office because of tasteful decor, they are more likely to respect your professionalism and believe you can deliver the services they need.

- *Reports and correspondence.*   The impression you make on paper is as important as the impression you make in person. Your reports and correspondence should always be neat, to the point, and without errors. If you use secretarial services, be sure the secretary has an eye for detail. Write-ins and spelling errors are inexcusable. In particular, with the availability of spell-check systems for word processing systems, there is no reason why even the worst speller should make mistakes. Correspondence filled with small errors, spelling or grammatical, can make clients nervous. After all, if you do not bring precision and neatness to your writing, why should you be expected to bring it to tax returns and accounting tasks?

- *Affiliated professional staff.*   If you have an office-sharing arrangement, be aware of how the other professionals in your office appear to your clients. Unfortunately, clients do not stop to consider whether the professionals who work near you also help with the services you provide; the assumption is that if you work in an office with others, they are somehow related to the work you do. Remember, office mates ultimately affect your image and practice success.

- *Administrative staff.* Your support staff is an extension of yourself. Neatly dressed and well-spoken receptionists, secretaries, and assistants help to further your professional image. On the other hand, inappropriate or untidy dress and curt behavior by support staff can deter potential clients from using you. Be sure you reinforce these values in your staff and reward them for positive client response.

- *Telephone image.* Developing a smooth, polite telephone style takes time. Sometimes practitioners are unaware they have a telephone persona that sounds cold or uninterested. Ask friends how you sound on the phone. When clients call, they should believe that you are happy to hear from them. Obviously, you cannot allow telephone time to impair your work schedule. Learn when to have a secretary take phone messages and how to end a conversation politely. If you must wait to answer phone messages, be sure you allow enough time to address the client's needs.

By using these tips to project a professional image, you establish client expectations. The best way to reinforce these expectations is by promptly delivering high-quality work. The image you build with clients extends into the professional community. This is important because it eventually leads to the best reinforcement you can receive, namely when a professional colleague says, "Yes, I know (your name). (He or she) is an outstanding CPA."

Face-to-Face Selling

All marketing efforts build toward the opportunity for you to talk with prospective clients face to face. But face-to-face selling can be intimidating, and many CPAs hesitate to take the initiative. In his book, *Selling Skills for CPAs: How to Bring in New Business* (1985), Charles Goldsmith points out some of the reasons why some CPAs hold back: "the possibility of rejection, risk of failure, and facing the unfamilar." They lack sales skills, find it embarrassing to discuss their own merits in person, and fear rejection.

Practice is the best method for overcoming possible intimidation or embarrassment. Experience comes with exposure to clients, but to avoid making mistakes and to gain confidence, try role playing with a colleague or friend. Have your counterpart play various types of potential clients so you can rehearse your approach.

Recording the session on videotape for analysis and review can be helpful. You may consider using a professional public speaking consultant to assist you in refining your delivery.

From practice comes a sense of how to handle various potential client scenarios such as the small business person looking for tax assistance, the person seeking the services of a CPA for the first time, and the person considering changing accountants. It is useful to develop standard scenarios for suggesting initial work in each situation. For example, you can offer to do a tax return for the first-time CPA client along with a review of the previous year's filed tax returns. For the small business person, you might offer a combination of controller and bookkeeping services or assistance in installing a computerized accounting system. For the client changing CPAs, ascertain why he or she is changing, then capitalize on the situation. Most often clients change because of inadequate services. By developing a well-devised response on how you will serve a potential client's needs, you move a get-to-know-each-other conversation into a closing situation.

You can significantly improve your comfort with a prospective client by researching his or her background. This enables you to hit important issues in your presentation and gives you material for questions. You can guide the conversation with questions that let the prospective client talk about himself or herself and give you the opportunity to make helpful, intelligent comments.

Marketing a Specialty Service

The accounting profession has been addressing various aspects of specialization for the last twenty years. At the present time, only an accredited personal financial specialty is recognized by the Specialization Accreditation Board of the AICPA. There are various recognized *de facto* specializations, such as construction accounting, litigation, and governmental auditing. How do you market a specialty?

The first step is to make sure you are well recognized by your peers and the users of your service. You gain recognition by teaching, lecturing, publishing, and concentrating on specific types of clients or services within your practice. Significant professional activities in your specialty also contribute. To get the word out to your target market, make your specialization one of the central themes in your marketing activities. Brochures and publications are beneficial because potential clients can learn more about you and your services. Also concentrate on using other CPAs as referral sources by representing your specialty as a synergistic complement to their general practice.

If you have an industry specialty, work to penetrate the support elements: industry trade associations, bankers, attorneys, insurance companies, and government agencies. By working with these groups and, when appropriate, becoming a referral source for them, you can develop a mutually satisfactory work and client-exchange relationship. Opportunities to make yourself more visible and gain more exposure to industry clients include joining support associations; publishing in trade periodicals; and becoming involved in efforts to establish standards, collect industrywide data, and build performance benchmarks. With any of these activities, be sure you receive credit for your work so that others recognize and appreciate your involvement.

Chapter 11

Managing Clients and Handling Fees

Determining the appropriate fee structure for your services is vital to successful practice development. Because there are many ways to compute charges, practitioners should approach this task with an eye on determining a fee structure that is fair, competitive, and easy to use. The most common methods for calculating charges are hourly rates and fixed fees. Practitioners also have the options of variable rate and relative value billing.

Estimating your costs and time to provide a particular service is difficult. A multitude of variables can increase or decrease productivity and out-of-pocket expenses. Typical factors that influence costs include change of personnel, competency of staff, condition of client records, change in service requirements, type of client demands, and modifications in tax laws and accounting standards.

In most cases, you want to follow the example of other successful accounting firms and set fees that are neither the highest in the business community nor the lowest. Because acquiring clients is a major concern, you may think it is wise to set low fees to entice new clients to your practice and later raise the fee structure to what you need. This approach gives your clients the wrong message and can even turn them away from you. Keep in mind that once fees are set, they should remain relatively stable for at least twelve months.

In addition to defining a reasonable fee structure, the practitioner must know how to discuss fees and summarize clearly in an engagement letter the services he or she will provide and what will be charged. Also, the practitioner must understand how to manage his or her time effectively.

This discussion begins with engagement letters and time management, since they are the precursors to the billing process. How to establish a fee structure, variable and relative value billing, contingent fees and commissions, fixed recurring fees, retainers, and undervaluing services are also discussed. You might want to take time to pinpoint those elements of managing clients that apply to you and the type of practice you plan to establish. By the end of the chapter, you should have a good idea of the fee structures that will best suit your particular needs.

Engagement Letters

Engagement letters state the terms of proposed work and serve as an agreement between the CPA and client. Before beginning a project, the CPA sends an engagement letter to the client and requests that it be signed, indicating agreement of the conditions cited within. This form of communication is beneficial because it prompts the practitioner to pull together an intelligent, thoughtful estimate of time and cost associated with a project and assures him or her that the client understands the terms.

When preparing an engagement letter, be sure to cover the following details:

1. Define the nature and extent of the work to be performed by respective parties, including the condition of the books and records.
2. Describe the objective as well as the projected results of the services that you will perform.
3. Clarify the rates, payment, and billing procedures related to the engagement.

By using engagement letters, you avoid misunderstandings and resolve issues before they become problems. This means you save time and money. Novice practitioners sometimes feel awkward about discussing fees at the outset of an engagement. Yet, this is an important aspect of client and practice management. If a client is uncomfortable with your fees and your estimate of hours and costs for services, you will quickly ascertain this and be able to discuss other options. Obviously, it is better to learn up front that a client does not like your terms than it is after beginning a project.

Unhappy clients tend to be reluctant clients who are not as likely to pay as those who signed their name to an agreement. (Appendix 2 provides some sample engagement letters.)

Time Management

Effective time management is fundamental to running a profitable business. Practitioners sell time and talent (TnT). Knowing where your TnT is used allows you to gauge your profitability. Regardless of how or how much you bill clients, you should always be able to tell how much time was spent on given services.

Keeping track of chargeable time is critical. But tracking nonchargeable time is also important. Record all of the hours you spend at work. Then, when you tally the monthly figures, discern where the nonchargeable time was spent. If you find you have too much nonchargeable time, ask yourself the following: Did I use my time as effectively as I could have? Could my nonchargeable TnT be delegated to someone less costly, thereby freeing me to do more chargeable work?

The following example illustrates the importance of time management to your bottom line. Assume that you are planning to gross $60,000 your first year and net $30,000. You charge $60 an hour for yourself and $20 an hour for your secretary. Given these basic figures, you now want to decide how to increase your profits. Your options include the following:

- Increase your billable time twelve minutes a day and you will increase your net profits by $3,000, or 10 percent of your goal of $30,000; increase your billable time by thirty minutes a day and you increase your net profits by $7,500, or 25 percent.

- Shift nonchargeable work to staff. A shift of hours between you and a secretary goes right to the bottom line if you have billable work to do. An increase of an hour a week in production can generate the same $3,000, or 10 percent of net.

- Charge for telephone calls, traveling, and research. With these additional items you easily pick up an additional fifteen minutes of chargeable time a day.

Because it is difficult to remember what you did during the day, let alone the day before, you should try to develop good time-recording habits, beginning with the first day of your practice. You need to log your activities as you complete them in sufficient detail to enable you to account clearly for that block of time. A good timekeeping system is fundamental to effective time management. See chapter 9 for information on establishing an effective timekeeping and billing system.

Fee Structure

How much should you charge? Many practitioners use the simple equation: x hours at y rate, plus out of pocket equals the billing amount. So, how do you decide your standard rate? This varies for each practitioner, depending on a number of factors. Because establishing a reasonable fee structure is critical to your success, be sure to review each carefully.

The first factor to consider is: What is standard in the profession? Firms bill from three to three and one-half times basic hourly compensation (2,080 divided into annual compensation), excluding overtime and bonuses. Some bill 2 percent of the monthly base pay for an hourly rate; others bill 1.75 percent of projected compensation, including overtime and bonuses. You should base your billing rate on an assumed salary or comparable salary to the practitioners in your area who possess skills similar to your own.

The second factor to consider is: What are your projected economic needs? Sufficient revenues must be generated to cover operating costs, debt service on borrowed funds, and personal income toward family needs. Obviously the goal is to have your practice become self-supporting as rapidly as possible with reasonable profits and adequate returns on investment.

The third factor to consider is: What is the competition charging? You can determine the answer to this through the following.

1. *Surveys.* A number of surveys exist that you can review to establish the average billing rates for sole practitioners and various-size firms. One that I recommend is The Texas Society's *National Report—Practice Management Survey.* This report is issued annually and includes information from approximately twenty states. You can also request a practice management report from your respective state CPA society, if your state participated in the survey.

2. *Informal exchanges.* Practice management groups offer excellent opportunities for the informal exchange of information. For example, MAP roundtable discussion groups sponsored by the MAP Committee of your state CPA society are ideal for discussing fees with other practitioners.

3. *Previous employment.* If you have previous work experience with accounting firms, you can use your former employer's billing rates as guidelines for setting your own fee structure.

4. *CPE courses.* CPE courses on practice management often address billing rates; sometimes the course instructor summarizes the participating firms' fee structures.

5. *Direct feedback.* Given the appropriate situation and conditions, you can be straightforward with competitors and ask what they are billing. Responses are usually candid and truthful.

Keep in mind that what the competition charges, particularly for traditional tax returns and periodic recurring services, may or may not be a good indicator of what you should charge; much depends upon each CPA's billing philosophy and quality of work. Therefore, be objective in your evaluation of competitors' rates.

Finally, the fourth factor to evaluate is: What are you worth? To evaluate this, consider the components listed below.

- *Overhead.* You need a clear picture of how much it costs to run your own practice and what you must earn to cover overhead and make projected profits.

- *Limited billing hours.* Since most practitioners only bill 50 to 70 percent of all work hours, the fee structure should be sufficient to offset nonbillable time.

- *Academic background.* Your education plays an important role in the skills, training, and experience you offer clients. The time and cost associated with your academic training is part of the fee structure you establish.

- *Continuing education.* Although your formal training in accounting may end with college or graduate school, you must still meet a CPE requirement and stay abreast of new developments in your profession. This is nonchargeable time, but it is time that ultimately benefits your clients.

- *Prior work experience.*   Clients are not merely paying for the immediate services they receive from you, they are also paying for your accumulated knowledge. Prior work experience is a significant determiner of fees.

- *Specialization.*   An expertise in particular accounting or tax services increases your value.

By considering these factors, you should be able to create reasonable billing rates. Remember, clients tend to accept your initial fee structure as a benchmark or standard against which they measure such matters as fee increases and referral of other clients to you. Although you can compromise on billed fees in the event of a dispute, you should stand firm with your rates.

Variable Billing Rates

Many beginning practitioners want to use a variable billing rate. Their rationale is that they are performing different levels of services, from typing reports or collating a return to principal-level work. From my own experience with starting practices and from surveying other sole practitioners, I do not recommend this type of billing. Too often, the tendency is to charge at the lower rate so as to avoid the never-ending overrun problem. Billing at substandard rates for your TnT can only cause problems. Practitioners who do it usually find themselves working evenings and weekends and indiscriminately accepting clients.

One way to handle the issue of how to charge for different levels of services is to select a standard rate for your most common services. Use this rate for all of your work. If in reviewing the accumulated time and charges you note you performed a substantial amount of work at a lower level, you can adjust for it. For example, if your normal rate is $90 per hour, and on a project you do some work that is normally performed by your assistant at $30 an hour, you might adjust your billing downward. However, remember that even though you are performing lower-level tasks, because of your knowledge and expertise you will be able to do the work rapidly and, at the same time, accumulate relevant data for later use. Accordingly, do not be too quick to make a downward adjustment.

Even though you want to avoid charging too little for your services, as can happen with variable rate billing, it is acceptable and fair to bill a premium for certain types or levels of work. For example, nonrepetitive, specialized work such as litigation support, mergers and acquisitions, contract negotiations, casualty-loss determination, tax planning and research, and MAS projects require a sophisticated level of skills. You are justified in charging higher rates for this work because it demands greater training, experience, and expertise than do the average accounting and tax services. And if you choose to concentrate or specialize in any of these services, your premium rate should become the standard rate.

Relative Value Billing

We hear a lot about relative value billing, which is essentially equating the billing to the perceived value of services rendered. It is not a common practice for those just starting in practice and, at least in my experience, is not that common for many established firms.

However, the AICPA and Federal Trade Commission (FTC) have tentatively approved a change in commissions and contingent fees that could have significant impact on fee arrangements and structuring, particularly as concerns relative value billing. Charging for specialized services will undoubtedly become more common. As a result, relative value billing may become a preferred method of billing by many practitioners.

As changes in standards occur, practitioners should keep alert to them and how they can be used to their advantage. Factors influencing the use of this billing method include—

- *Expertise.* The practitioner's skill, experience, and educational background are important considerations. If the CPA brings to a given job skills that extend beyond what the average CPA might have, this expertise is worth more than the standard fee.

- *Responsibility.* Different jobs require different levels of responsibility and risk. If the CPA assumes the burden of more responsibility and risk, it is appropriate to expect greater compensation.

- *Complexity.* The nature of a particular job or service and its related value to the client influences how much is expected of the CPA and the degree of his or her accountability. A complex negotiation, for example, demands more than standard skills from a practitioner and can result in high returns for the client. Depending upon the complexity of certain services it is fair to ask for greater remuneration.

- *Conditions.* If a job must be carried out under challenging work conditions such as a limited time frame, the practitioner should expect a higher fee.

Contingent Fees and Commissions

As noted, the AICPA and the FTC have tentatively agreed upon new rules whereby portions of fees could come in the form of commissions from a referred provider of a product or service. They also agreed upon revision of a standard that prohibited the acceptance of most engagements based on a contingent fee (billing based upon attained results). A significant qualifier is that the practitioner may not accept a commission involving certain "attest" clients. *Attest functions* are defined, for this purpose, as audit, review, certain compilation engagements, and examination of prospective financial information.

The lifting of these restrictions may have a significant impact on the accounting profession. For example, in addition to doing a client's tax return you may sell that client $100,000 worth of term life insurance if you believe he or she needs it. If you recommend a bank or mortgage company, you may receive a fee from the bank or company after the client completes a transaction. In unconventional specializations such as merger and acquisitions, financial planning, systems installation, and contract negotiations, you have more options for negotiating your compensation or fees, including compensation based on commissions and favorable results.

You should keep alert to the changes within your own state board of accountancy or state CPA society and consider how these changes can help you in your practice. Also, be aware of other potential constraints on your practice, such as regulatory licensing, malpractice insurance, and litigation concerns.

Fixed Recurring Fees or Retainers

One method practitioners use to price their services is to agree to perform a certain amount of work at a designated fee based on the needed services and conditions of client records. Coupled with this is a provision that allows a specified amount of time for contingencies or extra work. When it is used, there should be periodic reviews of the arrangement for adjustments by the client and practitioner.

A fixed fee or retainer arrangement is an attractive method for establishing regular income for the beginning practitioner, for the following reasons:

1. It is easy to sell, particularly if it is wrapped in a total service concept such as monthly financials, business and personal tax returns, quarterly payroll reports, and consultation, as needed, all for a fixed fee per month.

2. It is the type of service package offered by the sole practitioner's biggest competitors, namely noncertified practitioners, service bureaus, and moonlighters.

3. It provides steady monthly income and the potential for referrals.

Fixed fees can cause problems, particularly if the practitioner fails to price his or her service correctly. Problems to watch for include—

1. *Open-ended, all-encompassing arrangements.* These rarely work well for practitioners. Clients typically use the hours you projected, and then some.

2. *Underestimated fees.* If you attempt to increase your fees, your client may object to the change, and you may be tempted to perform fewer services or take inappropriate short cuts.

3. *Fear of losing clients.* Even though you may need to correct a miscalculation of fees by increasing prices, you may hesitate to do this and risk losing your client.

4. *Referrals based on bargain prices.* Clients who receive a bargain in a retainer arrangement often tell their friends and business acquaintances. This may mean a greater client base, but it may also mean an abundance of unprofitable work.

Although each practitioner must decide whether to use a fixed fee, I think it is useful to have some guidelines for establishing this type of an arrangement. An acceptable fixed fee or retainer arrangement is one in which you—

- Define the condition of the records you will accept, such as reconciled bank statements, balanced receipts and disbursements summary, and listed and classified payables.
- Specify end products or services in the arrangements such as compilations without disclosure, tax returns, quarterly payroll reports, and annual payroll reconciliations.
- Clarify how year-end work is to be billed. Will it be included in the monthly retainer or billed separately?
- Specify factors not included, such as IRS examinations, sales tax audits, personal tax returns, and bank loan proposals.
- Specify the amount of time allotted for conferences, questions, and year-end planning. This should be a cushion or contingency factor.
- Make a provision for a review of arrangements and their modification if necessary. This provides flexibility to maneuver if you discover you underestimated costs.

Undervaluing Services

Without question, it is easier to sell your services when your fees are substantially lower than the prevailing market. Practitioners who do this often find they have more clients than they can handle. However, when you establish a practice by undervaluing your services, you also create problems that may cause long-term difficulties, such as the following:

1. You face the potential inability to raise fees in subsequent years because of resistance from clients who now expect low fees.
2. You become out of touch with what the competition is charging; because you are uninformed, you may continue to quote fees much lower than necessary.
3. You become incapable of attracting sophisticated clients. Clients who have the money to pay more for services are not as easily influenced by a low fee as they are by quality, competence, and timely service.
4. Quality of your service and work is more likely to be compromised. There are only two alternatives for a practitioner

whose practice shows substandard profits, either work more hours or reduce the quality of the services offered.

Undervaluing services can also take the form of offering special concessions to start-up businesses. Practitioners are often eager to obtain work from novice companies because getting in at the ground floor allows them to establish a niche in the company. This could be rewarding for you, particularly if the company does well and grows quickly. However, you also risk payment problems from those companies that are unsuccessful, and there is no guarantee that successful firms will stay with you as they grow. I recommend that you consider working with start-up businesses by charging your standard rate, but allowing the company to pay 75 percent at the completion of the services and the remaining 25 percent over time. Terms and penalties for late payment (beyond your specified extended payment schedule) must be specified in your engagement letter. With this method, the clients know your standard billing rate and expect to advance to regular payment terms as they get on their feet.

If you feel it is worth your time and expense to absorb some of the costs for a start-up company, let the client know this deferment of costs is a one-time deal and you expect full payment for future services. Though I do not recommend doing this on a regular basis, there are times it is worth waiving some costs to establish yourself with a company and potentially benefit from long-term rewards and profits.

Chapter 12

Billing and Collection Techniques

Billing and collection time is a time when the practitioner should feel proud of his or her work and look forward to the monetary rewards. For many practitioners, however, billing and collection can be a daunting task. Sometimes it is because practitioners are embarrassed to talk about money, or they have not accepted that they are worth the fees they charge. Other times it is because collections may require aggressive tactics to achieve the desired result. For these reasons, it is important that before starting a practice you decide which of the various billing and collection procedures you want to use. Even if you have an office staff that handles the actual billing details, well-defined guidelines help facilitate procuring payment for your services.

This chapter examines good billing techniques, service charges, bank credit cards, what to do when the client does not pay, suing for fees, and coping with major cost overruns.

Effective Billing Techniques

One good billing technique is knowing when you should ask for a retainer; that is, receiving money in advance of services rendered instead of billing while the work is in progress or at the completion of a project. The following work commonly lends itself to a retainer arrangement:

- Litigation support
- Previously unfiled tax returns
- Nonclient tax examinations

- Loan proposals
- Private placements
- Extensive research projects
- Tax fraud cases
- Clients still owing for prior services
- Clients who previously disputed or compromised a prior billing
- High-risk engagements

In cases where you feel it is appropriate to require a retainer because of perceived risks within the engagement or with the client, ask yourself, Do I really want to undertake this project or client? Even though you may be paid in advance, and paid well, there is always the potential of adverse results. Your reputation can be damaged if you associate with unethical clients, and litigation can quickly overcome any anticipated monetary rewards.

Some CPAs routinely ask for a retainer arrangement with new clients. It improves cash flow, makes the client aware of the necessity to pay for services when rendered, and reduces losses from uncollected services. However, this action is perceived by some as being too aggressive and can discourage clients from using you. Weigh each situation on its own merit. If you have a comfortable relationship with your client, working on a retainer basis may be satisfactory for both parties.

Another good billing technique is to know how to expedite billing and collections. Sole practitioners face the constant pressure of maintaining adequate cash flow for running their practices. Therefore, the quicker you can procure outstanding receivables, the better your ability to manage your business and direct its growth. The following situations offer good opportunities for speedy billing and payments.

1. *Completion of individual tax returns.* When you or your secretary call clients regarding completed tax returns, inform them of your final fee. Although it is not necessary to schedule an exit conference for nominal or moderate returns, you may want to be in the office in case the client has any questions. Payment should be made at the time of the pickup.

2. *Appointments with recurring fixed-fee clients.* When these clients bring their records to you, they should be encouraged to bring the monthly or periodic fee also.

3. *Scheduled exit conferences.* When you schedule an exit conference to deliver a completed service or product, ask in advance that the client have your payment ready for you. This arrangement should have been clearly stated in the engagement letter.

4. *Completion of work.* Whether you have an exit conference, hand-deliver work, or mail it, you can establish a policy of "payment upon completion." Doctors, dentists, attorneys, and even ministers are all paid before or at the time a service is rendered and completed; CPAs are free to entertain this option as well. If you choose to use this policy, let clients know before beginning any project. Also, realize some may not like this policy and may choose to find another CPA for their work.

A third good billing technique is knowing how to bill when you do not use a retainer arrangement or receive payment upon completion of work. I recommend the following procedures:

1. At a minimum, bill monthly. Biweekly or semimonthly billing is also acceptable. Mail your invoices the next day after the billing cycle ends, never delay getting your invoice to your clients. Typically, payment is due within thirty days after billing.

2. Whenever practical, bill work in process. This helps to negate the overall shock of a large bill at the end of a project and eases your own cash flow.

3. Provide sufficient detail on your billing so that the client understands the nature of the services provided and the time frame being billed. Although firms vary on the amount of itemization to use on bills, a good rule of thumb is to ask yourself what type of information and itemization you want to see on a bill from someone whose services you used. Refer to your timekeeping system for descriptions of the services provided.

4. Separate out-of-pocket expenses such as travel, photocopies, luncheons, and support-staff time on your invoice.

5. Verify that your billing is consistent with the terms of the engagement letter. Any deviations should be adequately explained.

Service Charges, Credit Cards, and Discounts

It is increasingly common for CPA firms to apply a service charge on past-due bills. Even though collection of the amount is not assured, the appearance of the service charge frequently prompts the client to pay.

Other professionals such as doctors, dentists, and attorneys allow credit card charging as a convenient, on-the-spot form of payment. CPAs are slowly following suit. Now, with the competition offering more and more services and the costs of running a small business requiring fast cash turnaround, practitioners would be wise to provide this option for their clients.

Some firms offer discounts for prompt payment and for work performed in off-season. In some instances firms reduce fees for a tax return that is completed before March 1. As a sole practitioner you can consider these options, remembering that if you undervalue your services too much through discounts, you must make up the difference with an increase in workload, which usually means increasing your client base.

When the Client Does Not Pay

CPAs, as all professionals, must deal with the frustrating problem of how to handle clients who refuse to pay or cannot pay. Usually, the reason why the client has not paid is that a bill was not sent or was lost in the mail, the client disputes the amount charged, the client lacks funds, or the client never felt a commitment to pay.

A prompt billing reminder by statement will solve the question of whether the bill has been received. If you suspect the client disputes the bill or has insufficient funds, your only option is personal contact—pick up the phone and call your client. Be cordial but firm. Ask why you have not received payment. Then, discuss methods for resolving the unpaid bill.

Should conflicts over billing be resolved by compromise? Two schools of thought exist. One says to stand firm and demand you receive payment as presented on your bill; the other recommends negotiating a compromise. From my own experience, I prefer the latter view. First, it is better to receive some payment than none at all. And second, the amount of time and effort you may have to devote to procuring payment can quickly eat away financial gains.

If you choose to compromise, do not acknowledge any diminution of the value of the services you rendered. Make the adjustment with a written statement specifying that you are doing that as a result of the client's financial situation, lack of communication between the parties, or for whatever other reason that allows you to remain in the driver's seat as the one choosing to make the concession. In addition, be certain to reaffirm that this adjustment is a one-time occurrence and is not standard policy, to preclude the client from attempting to get a similar concession in later years.

When a compromise is made, usually it is based on collecting the agreed-upon amount immediately or receiving secured notes or other collateral. During or after settlement, decide the extent of further credit extension and future services. Most important, identify the causes for the client not paying, particularly if it is a dispute, so that both parties can work to prevent the situation in the future.

For those situations in which clients do not have the funds to pay, it is imperative that you inform them that your needs are just as important as those of their suppliers or employees, their taxes owed, and even their own take-home pay. Because you are thoroughly convinced of your own value to the client, you should have no problem persuading a client that you should be among the first of those to receive payment or even partial payment when funds become available.

If you are dubious about receiving immediate monetary payment, consider accepting a note or some other form of delayed and secured payment. Some CPAs make bartering arrangements—their receivable in exchange for the client's products. This type of arrangement is rarely publicized because it is somewhat embarrassing for the CPA and is even considered unprofessional by some. It is, however, one way of receiving something instead of nothing.

What do you do about those clients who did not intend to pay in the first place? Unfortunately, these situations you must often rack up to experience and try to learn from them. How could you anticipate this problem? Were you too eager to obtain the client and thereby failed to see indications of this lack of goodwill in your initial client investigation? What can you do to avoid a similar problem in the future? Whatever the error, try to identify it so you do not repeat it in the future.

Suing for Fees

There are occasions when the practitioner believes that suing the client for delinquent fees is a logical recourse. Suing can have negative consequences. Established practitioners express mixed feelings about this course of action; in most cases, they will not sue.

Why should the sole practitioner be cautious about initiating a lawsuit against a client?

1. A strong possibility always exists that a client will countersue, claiming you did not provide quality services or did not complete the work as contracted or scheduled.
2. Involving yourself in a legal action, even if you are the one initiating it, may affect your malpractice insurance, because insurance companies are wary of lawsuits that can backfire with countersuits.
3. The costs associated with a lawsuit may quickly negate any positive action in your favor.
4. The time and effort you devote to a lawsuit could be spent in financially productive endeavors. Time given a lawsuit is usually lost time in terms of financial gains.
5. The potential for negative publicity could harm your client base and future practice growth.
6. Even if you do win, you may discover that the client has no funds and that there is nothing to collect.

With these potentially negative repercussions, it is wise to evaluate your feelings and position before taking any action. Try to determine how the situation deteriorated to the point of a potential lawsuit. Was it due to lack of communication on your part or your client's? Did you fail to provide a timely or interim bill? Was your initial investigation of the client and the condition of his books and records inadequate? Are you confident you provided quality services on time and according to the arrangement outlined in an engagement letter? If you are confident you are without blame, and you are willing to risk the negatives of a lawsuit, then feel free to take the issue to a court of law.

Since a compromise is usually better for both parties, consider alternatives. For example, you might agree to an extended-term payout with the possibility of a settlement and service discontinuance. Or, you might accept a lower fee settlement. Again, the decision to compromise may not provide you with the recompense you deserve, but in the long run it may be a better solution than a lawsuit.

When CPAs who are involved in a fee dispute with a client, with litigation imminent, retain possession of their client's documents and records for leverage purposes, they are performing a discreditable act and are violating the AICPA Code of Professional Conduct, Rule 501. Any practitioner who participates in this type of activity not only harms his or her reputation but will lose clients and damage whatever practice potential exists.

Do you sue or don't you? If you find yourself in a potentially litigious situation with a client, evaluate all options. Collection agencies and small claims court sometimes achieve the same results, with much less time and money outlay. You may find it is best to accept the loss of fees. If, on the other hand, you choose to pursue a lawsuit, be sure you have a good attorney and weigh the anticipated rewards against the potentially negative consequences.

Billing for Major Cost Overruns

How do you handle major cost overruns? Should you bill for the additional time and costs or absorb the loss? As a beginning practitioner, you want to make a good impression on first-time clients and do not want to risk losing future business. However, if you attempt to absorb all major cost overruns, you will soon be working long hours for less than the minimum wage. I recommend whenever you realize there will be a major cost overrun, immediately communicate with the client. Explain why the problem occurred and negotiate additional fees. Do not ignore the situation; silence will only compound your difficulties with obtaining payment later.

How can you avoid major cost overruns? First, it is important to understand why they occur. The most commonly cited client-related reasons are poor working conditions, inadequate or incomplete client records, poorly trained client staff, poor communication, and ineffectual scheduling. The problems most frequently viewed as practitioner-related include inadequate job management, inordinate attention to technical detail, overauditing, excessive research, and efforts extending beyond the necessary. By being aware of both client- and practitioner-related problems, you can work to circumvent them.

When major cost overruns occur, conduct a thorough analysis of the situation to ascertain the reasons for the problem. Compare the actual time and results to what your engagement letter called for, both in the estimate of hours and client responsibility. If overruns exist for which you are at fault, eliminate that time from your billing. On the other hand, if there are client-related overruns, carefully detail the problems for discussion with the client.

Often a major cost overrun is the result of a disproportionate cost-to-fee relationship. This occurs in recurring work and in one-time work. If it happens on recurring work, the root of the problem is usually an unrealistic fee quotation, inefficient work production, or client-related issues. Beginning practitioners often face this problem because of their eagerness to obtain clients and their inexperience in calculating the amount of time and cost required to perform a given service. If this occurs, the practitioner should attempt to correct it as quickly as possible. Here are some steps that can be taken.

1. Correct client-related causes such as inadequate records, inefficient staff, and inappropriate client demands. By bringing work and time requirements in line with fees, it is often possible to correct a potential major cost overrun without impact on the fees.

2. Increase fees over a period of time. For example, add 5 percent a month for six months to justify the billing with the time and services provided.

3. Suggest that the client consider using another practitioner if he or she is unable or unwilling to accommodate either of the first two suggestions.

4. Terminate the client relationship as a last resort if the client is unwilling to accept and pay for the cost overruns.

Clients do not like surprises, particularly surprises on billings. The best defense against potential overrun situations is to provide interim billing with a letter describing your progress. When you must present a client with large and unusual bills, consider doing it in person so that you can explain the charges. Some CPAs disagree with this view, as they feel it might raise a question where none existed or might put the CPA on the defensive. If you are not comfortable with personal presentation, send the bill with an accompanying letter of explanation.

Needless to say, your client will be dissatisfied with the major cost overruns. Before you discuss the billing with him or her, you should ensure that you can address the following points:

1. Define any excesses that are your responsibility. Be reasonable on the degree of responsibility you assume—make sure it was your fault and that you are not merely trying to avoid confrontation.

2. Determine to your own satisfaction that the amount of the bill is fair and in line with fees generally charged by competitors.

3. Outline any excess costs caused by deficiencies associated with your client.

4. Approach the problem with a positive attitude about your worth, the reasons for the overrun, and the value you have provided to the client.

Chapter 13

Difficult Clients and Client Situations

Practitioners who worked for large firms might expect that because they had relatively few client problems in their previous work environment they will have few in their own practice. This is not always the case. Practitioners at large firms are often buffered from difficult clients.

As a sole practitioner, you must face difficult clients and situations on your own. What are the most common difficult client situations? Beginning CPAs most often cite resistance to fees, inappropriate client behavior, unanticipated complications, and refusal to pay. The optimum way to handle these problems is to avoid the problem before it occurs. If you take time to do a thorough client interview and investigation, you can often tell whether the client will be cooperative or not. However, it is unrealistic to assume that as a beginning practitioner you will turn down every client who seems apt to be difficult.

This chapter discusses how to cope with different clients and situations: to recognize a difficult or undesirable client; overcome fee resistance during the initial engagement meeting; handle client concerns about the scope and quality of your services; manage clients when you make mistakes; and dismiss undesirable clients from your practice.

Defining the Difficult or Undesirable Client

The initial client interview is a time of evaluation for both parties. Obviously, the primary focus is on you. You want to show the potential client you have the training and experience to handle his or her particular needs. But do not be so eager to sell yourself that you fail to assess the client. During the interview, investigate the client's background and needs to determine whether this will be a positive working relationship. Ask directly or try to discern through conversation answers to these questions:

1. How does the client feel about CPAs?

2. What are the client's views about tax authorities and bank requirements pertaining to financial statements?

3. How would the client characterize past accounting relationships? What kinds of problems, if any, did he or she encounter with prior accountants? Were there any particular fee disputes?

4. Is the client's overall financial position stable or possibly unstable?

5. How does the client perceive your role in his or her business future?

6. Would the client mind your contacting his or her previous accountant for access to past records? This is particularly appropriate if the potential engagement is for preparing financial statements for a lending institution or another third party.

If the client gives you permission to contact a previous accountant, follow through. You can verify access to past records and, if the practitioner is open to questions, you can obtain additional information concerning potential client-practitioner problems.

Before proposing an engagement, view the client's books and records and, if possible, talk to the prospective client's accounting staff. These are invaluable sources of information and, combined with the initial client interview, should give a fairly complete picture of your potential client-practitioner relationship.

Unfortunately, there are times when you begin working with a client but discover later that you made a mistake. The sooner you recognize this, the faster you can take action to remedy the situation, even if it means dismissing the client. Use these guidelines during your initial client interview, as well as later when you want to evaluate an established client relationship, to determine whether you are confronting a client who needs special handling or perhaps even to be dismissed.

- Consistently disputes fees or is tardy making payments
- Makes excessive demands upon you and your staff's time
- Asks for unrealistic schedules and sets unfair deadlines
- Is dishonest or of poor repute
- Procrastinates on his or her part of the agreement
- Lacks the business sophistication necessary to understand the CPA's role and function and the value of your services
- Cannot grasp the extent of responsibility and accountability assumed by a CPA and is unconcerned by the CPA's need to adhere to technical and professional standards
- Consistently furnishes incomplete or inaccurate data, fails to respond to the CPA's request to rework the data into a usable state
- Jumps from CPA to CPA or changes accounting firms on a regular basis and seemingly without justification
- Is a member of an industry that is declining or is held in poor esteem within the business community
- Refers frequently to legal recourse against CPAs, other professionals, or anyone of substance, or actually is frequently involved in legal entanglements with others

Remember, you are the one in control of the situation. You have the option to accept or dismiss a difficult client. By avoiding difficult clients, you have more time to focus on those clients who will help your practice become profitable.

Overcoming Fee Resistance

The discussion of fees is often the first difficulty a practitioner confronts with a new client. Open discussion and, when appropriate, negotiation are imperative. If the client has a problem with your fee structure, it is best to deal with this before the engagement begins, when only a minimum amount of time and effort has been invested. In the event you cannot resolve the issue, you and the client can part paths with amicable understanding.

Here are some suggestions to help overcome your client's initial fee objections.

1. Describe how others use your services to save money. To maintain client confidentiality, this should be a very general explanation of how accounting, tax, and financial services benefit clients.

2. Explain some of the intricacies of the CPA profession such as necessary training, both initial and ongoing, and the standards CPAs must meet. This is relevant if dealing with a client who has not used accountants extensively in the past. It also offers the opening you need to explain how your particular skills benefit the client's business.

3. Make a cursory review of your client's tax returns and books to pinpoint where your services can be used. Then, formulate money-saving questions and suggestions. For example, you might challenge the need for audits and reviews if compilations will suffice, provide useful information on time-saving computer systems, recommend different inventory controls, suggest new marketing tactics, and describe methods for increasing personnel efficiency. By giving specific examples of how money spent on your services transforms into savings or profit for the client, you cease to be viewed as a drain on business returns and instead become indispensable.

4. Ascertain that any objection to fees is not a cover for some other objection, such as not wanting to pay taxes.

5. Point out how the client's business requires the expertise of highly qualified, competent professionals. Then describe how your accounting, tax, and financial skills can best benefit your client's business. This approach works particularly well for clients whose services or products are among the better ones in their field. Clients who are proud of their business reputation want to maintain high quality by using professionals who also have good reputations.

Handling Concerns About Scope of Services

Sole practitioners cannot expect to offer the scope and quality of services a large firm provides. For many practitioners, this is a major concern; they believe it to be a disadvantage. After all, how can one person compete against firms employing numerous accountants with diverse skills and training? First, I think it is important to recognize that you are not competing against larger firms. As a sole practitioner you have a limited range of services to offer. Clients understand this. If they need a broad range of expertise, they seek out a large firm where they can draw upon the skills of many individuals.

Does this mean you can hope to attract only clients of lower economic means and needs? Not at all. You offer the advantage of being less expensive than a large firm and of providing more individualized attention. These features are attractive and help draw clients with complex needs to you.

How do you neutralize the differences between a large firm and your own practice and entice clients to use you? Good marketing techniques and an aggressive attitude are characteristic of successful practitioners. Before marketing your services, have a realistic view of your limitations. Clients have every right to become difficult if you assured them you could handle their work needs and they later learn you are not trained or equipped to do it.

Once you define your limitations, do your best to overcome them. For example, assume you become a general service practitioner, offering business services including tax preparation and periodic accounting services through review statements and that you do not do audits. One of your clients needs an audit. What do you do? If you do some advance planning, you can line up an accounting firm to handle the audit work. By establishing a network of cooperative exchanges with other CPAs and CPA firms, you provide your clients with the breadth of services they need. In this situation you are akin to the "family doctor," handling most of the client's needs but seeking counsel or referring to others when beyond your professional scope of services.

To minimize the risk of losing clients to the firm that provides a particular service, draw up an agreement regarding client conversion. The legality of such agreements depends on local statutes. Although you do not own a client, presumably you could enter into an agreement with another CPA limiting his or her services to those referred. Also the agreement, either written or verbal, dictates the understanding between the parties. If a CPA firm fails to adhere to agreed-upon conditions, it risks damage to its reputation.

Eventually, some of your clients might outgrow your firm and need to find a larger one. Even in this situation, do not assume that you lost to the competition. Take a positive stand. If you maintain an amicable relationship with the client and guide him or her to a capable firm, you may retain a portion of the work. If not, you may at least have won a loyal client-referral source.

Managing Clients When You Make a Mistake

CPAs do make mistakes. Some mistakes are irritating and embarrassing; others are expensive to both the practitioner and the client. When a mistake occurs that is merely embarrassing, such as missing an appointment, take responsibility for it and put it behind you as quickly as possible. Try to prevent the mistake from happening again and do all you can to reassure the client that you are competent and professional, albeit human.

When a mistake goes beyond embarrassment to being either an irritant or an added expense for the client—for example, penalties imposed on returns, or missing filing deadlines—you face a more difficult situation. In most cases you can expect to be the scapegoat for the mistake, even though it may result from incorrect or inadequate information or errors made by the client's staff. How should you handle this situation? Obviously, there is a high probability you will lose the client if you do not resolve the problem quickly and satisfactorily. First, determine why the problem happened. Then, discuss it calmly with the client. If it is your fault, take appropriate action to remedy the situation. On the other hand, if it is the client's fault, describe the problem clearly and without ascribing blame. Some clients will, unfortunately, be uninterested in discussing the problem and want only to ascertain that you take full responsibility for the mistake. Clients who behave in this manner are undesirable clients and should be weeded out of your practice.

Finally, there are occasions when mistakes go beyond being irritants and evoke malpractice claims. If you find yourself confronting an error that could result in a malpractice claim, I strongly recommend that you act conservatively and defensively: Notify your attorney or insurance carrier. Note this excerpt from section 217 of the *MAP Handbook* that addresses how to protect yourself against malpractice losses:

> One of the most traumatic experiences in the life of a CPA occurs when the firm is served with a summons and complaint involving

professional work that was performed for a client. Even firms with the most comprehensive controls, highly qualified personnel, quality clients, and complete insurance protection may expect to be sued sometime. Whether groundless or not, and whether the accusation is something covered by insurance or not (plaintiff's attorney will build his case to encompass both included and excluded acts), the claim must be defended. When faced with a claim, the following steps should be taken:

- Notify the insurance company IMMEDIATELY that there has been, or may be, a claim.
- Make no admissions, attempt no negotiations, and make no commitments, unless specifically authorized to do so by the insurance company.
- Notify and keep the firm attorney informed.
- Appoint someone in the firm, preferably someone not involved with the engagement, to coordinate communications and assemble and safeguard documents as directed by the firm attorney.
- Consult with the firm attorney concerning the extent and content of any internal memoranda relating to the matter BEFORE creating them.
- Keep everyone in the firm briefed on the status of the claim.
- Interview anyone connected with the engagement and explore their recollection of the circumstances (document these interviews in writing or use a tape recorder).
- Be completely frank with the insurance company; cooperate and provide all assistance requested.

Should the claim turn out to be within the amount of the deductible clause in the policy, then all steps above apply to the firm's attorney.

The experience of defending against a malpractice suit can be time-consuming, threatening, harmful to reputations, expensive (either directly or indirectly), and exasperating. It is extremely difficult to agree to settle a case when you may be right, but the costs of defense and the possibility of losing may outweigh the benefits of contesting. The insurance company will know when to fight and when to settle.

Dismissing, or "Firing," Undesirable Clients

The initial client interview lets you avoid contracting with clients who could prove to be difficult or undesirable. However, as an eager sole practitioner, you will undoubtedly acquire clients you would do better without. When this happens, I recommend you take the necessary steps to bring the clients up to the level of what you understand to be a standard relationship. If this is not possible, terminate your association with them.

How do you assess a client to determine whether you should continue your association or not? Use of a written client evaluation form or questionnaire will be helpful. Appendix 5 contains an evaluation form from section 204 of the *MAP Handbook*. I suggest that you use that written appraisal method for *all* of your clients. Not only do you define difficult clients, but you also determine clients to single out and recognize for their contribution to your practice.

If you have a client who sits on the edge of your consideration as an undesirable client, consider the following options:

- Wait to take action if you think there may be some improvement. After making an effort to correct the problem through subtle suggestions, place the client on an "internal probation" list, and reassess the situation after a predetermined period of time.

- Initiate a meeting with the client to discuss your concerns. You might find the client has concerns of his or her own that are getting in the way of an amicable work relationship. Sometimes joint corrective action helps alleviate a problem.

- Terminate the relationship. In many situations both the practitioner and the client are better served by this solution. One of the surprising results practitioners often find in their evaluation of clients is that a high percentage of problems with a practice are often created by a small percentage of clients. If you dismiss, or "fire," the problem clients, your practice becomes more efficient and more profitable.

Part V

Anticipating the Future

Chapter 14

Planning for Growth

One of the questions most frequently asked at the conclusion of my CPE course, "Starting Your Own CPA Firm," is, "What changes should I expect in the second, third, and fourth years of my practice?" Although each practice has its own style and rate of growth, depending upon location, services offered, client base, and diverse economic factors, there are certain benchmarks that usually occur during the initial years of development. These include exceeding $100,000 in gross billings, hiring professional staff, upgrading office facilities, and negotiating a merger with other CPAs.

How do you assure you are doing what you should to foster growth? First, it is important to understand that what happens in the future is largely dictated by what you do at the conception of your practice. The foundation you lay prepares the way for success. This is true whether you want to grow or simply maintain a profitable quality practice.

With industry data indicating that there is greater profitability with growth, many sole practitioners start their practices with the intention of expanding as soon as they establish a solid client base. If you have growth as a desired goal or, at least, as an option to consider, then your planning should start now.

Topics featured in this chapter are how to determine if growth is right for you, quality of growth versus quantity, the hiring of staff, and preparing a practice continuation agreement. Even if you think the issue of growth is too far removed from the immediate concern of starting your practice, consider the idea for a moment now. Practitioners are often surprised how quickly their initial goals and dreams change to become larger and more comprehensive. By having a sound understanding of future possibilities you are better able to recognize and seize opportunities that can further your practice.

Is Growth Right for You?

Success is often equated with growth, and beginning practitioners assume that once they achieve profitability they should expand. Before making this decision, however, have a clear idea of how you define success. Is success making money? Is it enjoying a fine reputation? Is it managing your practice in such a way that you are not required to work unreasonably long hours and, therefore, have time for personal and family interests? In most cases, success is a combination of all three, profitability, reputation, and controlled hours. But how you weigh each of these factors is the true determiner of success as you see it.

Understanding what your own view of success is and not allowing yourself to be swayed by peer or societal pressure are fundamental to planning your practice growth. For some, remaining a sole practitioner is the best option, whereas for others developing a practice into a multidimensional firm is a logical choice. Each approach does constitute success, provided it is the path you choose to take.

Look at other practitioners you respect and practices that you admire. Get an image of what you want to emulate. Two firms I watched grow and change over the years exemplify how different a practice development can be and how personal and professional factors can influence growth. One firm has two partners, six professional staff, and support staff. It generates approximately $200,000 net per partner per year while requiring approximately 2,400 hours per year from each partner. The firm is a little over ten years old and enjoys a fine reputation in its community. The other firm also has two partners but does not employ any professional staff. It specializes in several tax services, offers no accounting services, and generates approximately $100,000 net per partner per year with an annual commitment of 2,000 hours per partner. This firm is five years old, and the partners are committed to a more relaxed lifestyle, including no more than fifty hours per week during tax season and thirty-two to thirty-six hours per week in nonseason. The firm averages 1,250 chargeable hours per partner.

Both of these firms are successful, but not merely because of the bottom line returns. The partners in the firms had well-defined goals and methodically carried out their plan of action. When opportunities for growth occurred, they knew which directions to take; they guided their own destinies without indecision.

As a beginning practitioner you face the same type of choices the CPAs in the above examples faced. By consciously deciding whether you want to expand or remain small and by establishing guidelines for the future, you can help ensure your practice grows in the manner you want.

Quality of Growth vs. Quantity

Sometimes practitioners find their services filling a need not previously addressed. When this happens, establishing a client base is easy, perhaps too easy. As an eager sole practitioner, it is unlikely you will turn down clients, unless they are undesirable ones. But, in turn, it is possible to find yourself with more work than you can realistically do.

What is the key to handling growth? Do you sacrifice quality for quantity? The obvious answer is no. However, to avoid this problem, you must be aware of why it occurs. Since most practitioners are first and foremost concerned with obtaining clients, it is easy to get carried away committing your hours to low-fee, high-demand clients. But the more you do this, the more clients you need to achieve profitability, lessening your chance of obtaining quality clients.

To help encourage quality growth, it is important to set minimum client standards. As stated in chapter 13, predetermining standards for clients helps you differentiate between those you should and should not acquire. In addition, if you have a clear picture of what is an optimum client, you can direct your marketing efforts accordingly. Even though initially you cannot pick and choose, you can be more discriminating as your practice grows.

Periodically reevaluating your practice strategies also enhances quality growth. If you sacrificed initial goals and standards for the sake of establishing a client base, this assessment process is extremely important. Define where you made trade-offs, then ask yourself, What do I need to do to get back on track? On the other hand, if you are satisfactorily pursuing the objectives you set for yourself, use this reevaluation process to outline new avenues for furthering your practice development.

In mergers or associations with other accounting firms for the purpose of growth, the issue of quality is critical. Increasing the size of a practice creates larger profit only if the growth is qualitative. Frequently practitioners who merge or associate with another firm discover that the quality in their own practice, which they worked hard to establish, is undermined by the new relationship.

The risks in this type of growth are high. Although statistics are not available on the results of mergers and acquisitions of accounting firms, my experience suggests there are probably as many that do not work out as those that do. Even when the new affiliations do work, quality is often jeopardized or sacrificed. If you want to grow in this manner, I suggest you do a thorough analysis of the firm with which you want to merge or associate.

Hiring Professional Staff

As I mentioned in the beginning of this chapter, certain benchmarks usually occur in the first few years of practice, and reaching a yearly gross of $100,000 ranks as one of the most significant. One way to achieve this is to have 1,400 chargeable hours at $70 an hour. This is difficult to do, even with adequate client demand, unless you have support staff who perform your administrative duties and other nonchargeable functions. If you are interested in growth, I feel it is imperative you hire part-time or full-time support staff at the start of your practice. By shifting low-level work to your staff, you can take advantage of growth opportunities without forfeiting quality. (Chapter 9 discusses the benefits of having support staff.)

The second most significant benchmark for beginning practitioners is hiring professional staff. Although most starting practitioners do not address this issue until the second or third year of practice, the more aggressive, and frequently more successful, practitioners look for professional staff from the start.

The key consideration in hiring professional staff is not who but *when*. You should hire before reaching the point at which you are overburdened with both chargeable and administrative time requirements. A good rule of thumb is that when you have 600 to

1,000 hours of work that can shift to another professional, your returns will be greater than your costs. Additional factors are the potential of the new professional to bring in clients, your enhanced image and increased visibility in the community, and the reward of more time to market and obtain a larger client base.

Make your decision to hire professional staff only after an objective analysis of the growth and fee structure, including adequate profitability of your practice. Unquestionably, professional staff take away some of your chargeable hours as well as require supervision and administrative support. In weighing the pros and cons, ask yourself the following: If I increase my fees instead of hiring another professional, will I achieve the same objective? Can I generate enough new clients to keep the new member busy and profitable? Will there be other increases in expenses besides the cost for the new professional, such as malpractice insurance and space needs, that cannot be recovered under the current fee structure?

If after your analysis of the situation you decide to hire professional staff, take time to investigate the backgrounds of potential candidates. Check all possible references and, if necessary, make the initial employment contract conditional for the first thirty to sixty days. If there are any serious problems during the early stages of employment, take immediate action. You pay a high price to obtain professional help, and there is no point in saddling yourself with someone who is difficult to work with or cannot handle the duties and assignments you delegate.

What if you need additional help but you cannot afford another professional? You can consider—

1. *Support staff.* Use your support staff at the highest level possible. If you take time to train them in more sophisticated tasks you can transfer administrative and operational work to them. Support staff work for clients is billable. By having lower level staff handle routine tasks, you are free to do higher level chargeable work or spend time marketing your services. Also, allocate money for additional staff training. Consider college and adult education courses and staff training through state CPA society programs. These increase your staff's capabilities and usefulness.

2. *Office and staff sharing.* Instead of hiring full-time staff, look at office or staff sharing. Often others in your same

situation are eager to cut costs by splitting the services of a staff member. Be aware that if you cannot guarantee hours, you probably have to pay a premium for the hours you use. Although this is not optimum, it is better than hiring a full-time staff when you only have enough work for a part-time employee.

3. *Contract staff.* You can frequently hire contract staff for approximately 40 percent of what you can bill for them. The risks associated with this are that you do not know the quality of their work, and contract staff are usually interested in finding full-time work and may, consequently, be available only for an indeterminate period.

4. *Part-time staff with previous accounting experience.* People previously employed as staff for accounting firms and not currently in the job market are excellent potential employees. Individuals who are raising families but still want to remain professionally active and current as well as those who have recently retired from the profession are good options. If you offer an attractive package, such as limited seasonal work and flexible hours, you might gain valuable employees. In addition, you benefit from their prior work experience. To seek out these potential employees, ask former coworkers, place advertisements in state CPA society publications, and contact other CPAs.

Preparing a Practice Continuation Agreement

Ideally, a practice continuation agreement should be drawn up when you establish your practice. This agreement is an action plan that in the event of your death or permanent disability provides for the assumption and purchase of your practice by another CPA or in the event of a short-term disability arranges to have your clients temporarily serviced by another CPA firm.

Although preparing a practice continuation agreement requires time and effort, it is a commitment well invested. With such an agreement in place you are assured that both the business interests of your clients and the financial interest of your family are protected should death or disability deprive you of the ability to manage your practice.

Chapter 15

Nurturing Your Professional and Personal Development

Starting your own CPA firm is an exciting adventure and can be one of the most rewarding experiences of your professional career. But as with any undertaking that demands a high output of energy and concentration, there is the danger of losing yourself in the daily work and neglecting your personal and professional growth. While you establish your practice, begin to allocate time for your own development. Actively pursue professional and technical reading, continuing education courses, conferences, meetings and seminars, professional organizations, and other forms of professional expression. Each of these develop your professional expertise and further your personal growth.

Professional and Technical Reading

Schedule time for professional and technical reading. The continuous changes in tax laws, regulations, and rulings make it imperative that CPAs keep abreast of what is happening in their respective fields. However, because of the proliferation of information, you must be selective about what you read. You need to be current on the issues and trends affecting the business community and the accounting profession. Concentrate on issues critical to your practice. Choose two or three publications to speed read each week. For example, in the tax field, your tax services' periodic updates are mandatory. Tax periodicals such as *The Tax Advisor, The Journal of Taxation*, and *Taxation for Accountants* are published on a regular basis. *The Journal of Accountancy* offers up-to-date information on the profession, as well as articles of interest to practitioners through its various departments such as the "Practitioner's Forum." *The Practicing CPA*, a publication of the AICPA, whose sole objective is to provide practice management advice to the local practitioner, is also suggested reading for the new practitioner, as is the *Practical Accountant*, a practice-oriented publication dealing with everyday issues of practice management. Other reading might include your local business publications and regional issues of the *Wall Street Journal*.

Continuing Education

In most states the continuing education requirement is forty hours a year. Continuing professional education (CPE) offers an excellent opportunity to improve traditional accounting skills in tax, auditing, and accounting; to learn current and new practice management techniques; and to further knowledge in growing fields, such as financial planning and computers. CPE courses are also useful for exchanging ideas and opinions with your peers and for keeping current with the direction of the profession. Even though your primary concern is running your new business, take time each year to choose carefully the CPE courses to attend.

Conferences, Meetings, and Seminars

The AICPA, state societies, and professional associations offer various conferences, meetings, and seminars. Some of these are beneficial to the new practitioner. They include—

- MAP roundtable discussion groups. Contact your state society MAP committee for information on this forum.
- The AICPA Small Firm conference, offered twice a year throughout the country. Mailings are sent by the AICPA to all small firms, but contact the AICPA Industry and Practice Management Division if you do not receive a notice.
- State society MAP conferences and local practitioners or small firm conferences. These are found through your state society CPE listings.
- MAS, MAP, professional issues discussion groups, computer user's group, estate planning councils, and specialty groups such as litigation support discussion groups. Again, locate these through your state society.

Like formal CPE courses, these conferences, meetings, and seminars offer the opportunity for professional growth, exchanges of ideas, and professional evaluation.

Professional Organizations

Even though it is difficult to take time from your practice, it is a worthwhile investment to become involved in professional organizations. The initial involvement in professional activities for state societies or the AICPA is typically not too burdensome. Consider serving on committees while your practice is maturing, then when you feel you have time take on more responsible positions as a committee chair and as a member of a task force. Participation in professional organizations is an excellent way to further your outside contacts.

The AICPA offers its members a wide range of services. Appendix 7 identifies those services of particular interest to the local practitioner.

Other Forms of Professional and Personal Expression

Professional and technical writing offers another avenue for expression and enhancement of your professional image. My first published article appeared in the *Journal of Accountancy* in June 1983. The editor of the journal called and asked me to write an article on starting your own practice. Although I had not considered writing for national periodicals before, I discovered this form of expression gave me satisfaction and was an excellent vehicle for defining my thoughts. Whether you enjoy writing or not, I recommend this type of endeavor for increasing your exposure and for developing your communication skills.

Teaching also increases communication skills and gives the opportunity to further your professional image. Local colleges are often interested in CPAs teaching part-time. In addition, teaching continuing professional education courses for state societies offers both expressive and financial remuneration.

Finally, public speaking and lectures on specialties or concerns can be personally and financially rewarding. You can arrange your speaking engagements through the speakers bureau at your state society or by marketing yourself through the SBA, chambers of commerce, banks, and Toastmasters International.

Epilogue

The decision to start a practice is not for everyone. I have had participants in my group study class who have repeated the course as much as ten years later, still not knowing if it is the right decision. For others, it has been the best choice possible.

You have been given a great deal of information in the text, along with direction about avenues to explore for further help. By applying what I have said in the book to your own facts and situation, you will be able to make an intelligent assessment.

A starting point for the assessment is to complete the checklist in appendix 1, a series of sixty-two questions serving as a brief summary of the text and a challenge to your preparation for being *On Your Own!*

GOOD LUCK!!

Checklist for Starting Your Own Firm

The following questions cover the main issues dealt with in this book related to starting a practice. Questions correlate to the respective chapters in order to help your review your responses. If you respond in the negative, you can then review that portion of the chapter, or all of it.

	Yes	No	N/A

Chapter 1—Going Solo

1. Have I adequately determined my reasons for wanting to start my own firm, and are my reasons based upon a well-thought-out analysis of my situation?

2. Have I placed the potential of financial gain of starting my own firm in the proper perspective after a realistic assessment?

Chapter 2—Profile of a Successful Sole Practitioner

3. Can I give myself satisfactory grades in the following qualifications necessary to succeed in my own business?

   • Academic and professional experiences

   • Defined goals and standards

   • Work skills and habits

   • Attitude and demeanor

4. Have I designed a plan to overcome my perceived weaknesses or deficiencies in the qualifications listed in question 3?

	Yes	No	N/A

Chapter 3—Critical Considerations

5. Have I planned and budgeted my hours and anticipated my financial needs?

6. Have I properly assessed the competition and determined how to obtain a sufficient client base?

7. Do I know an effective method for accounting for my time?

8. Have I considered the loss of benefits and the increase in expenses associated with the move into my own firm?

9. Does my family realize the new undertaking will take time and involvement on their part as well as mine?

10. Am I alert to the potential pitfalls of premature or inappropriate mergers and associations with other CPAs or firms?

Chapter 4—Generalist or Specialist?

11. Have I determined what services I will offer, along with those services I will not try to compete in?

12. Have I given thought to a specialization or concentration of services or industries within my practice?

13. If I have the skills, training, and background necessary to have a specialty, have I developed plans to take advantage of this?

14. Whether generalist or specialist, have I adequately identified my target market?

Chapter 5—To Buy or Not to Buy?

15. Have I carefully weighed the advantages and disadvantages of buying and not buying a practice?

16. In deciding to buy a practice, have I considered carefully my technical skills, practice management style, and personal characteristics?

	Yes	*No*	*N/A*

17. Have I considered that regardless of the price asked and the demand for available practices, the acquisition must still make economic sense and be based on a logical budget or plan that includes projected loss of clients? _____ _____ _____

18. Have I considered the likelihood that some clients will remain for a reasonable period of time after the acquisition and some will not? _____ _____ _____

Chapter 6—Which Form of Organization for Your Practice?

19. Have I weighed the advantages and disadvantages of sole proprietorship, partnership, office sharing, and incorporation and determined which is best for me? _____ _____ _____

Chapter 7—Financing Your Business

20. Have I prepared a business plan even if I do not need to seek outside financing? _____ _____ _____

21. Have I been realistic in projecting my costs and expenses and estimating my income? _____ _____ _____

22. Have I calculated the benefits lost and cost incurred that were previously paid by an employer but are now my responsibility as a sole practitioner? _____ _____ _____

23. Is my family aware of the financial aspects of starting my own practice? _____ _____ _____

24. If I am unable to obtain adequate financing, will I postpone my decision to start my own practice until my financial position is stronger? _____ _____ _____

Chapter 8—Choosing an Office Location

25. Does the location I've chosen serve my target market? _____ _____ _____

26. Have I carefully weighed the advantages and disadvantages of working out of a home office? _____ _____ _____

	Yes	No	N/A

27. Have I considered the advantages and disadvantages of office sharing with another CPA or other professional?

28. Does the office location I'm considering reflect the proper image and offer convenience and accessibility?

Chapter 9—Operational Issues

29. Have I carefully weighed all of the advantages of hiring administrative staff at the inception of my practice?

30. Can I use to my advantage the current state of technology used in the accounting profession?

31. Have I developed a clear and concise set of standards and policies relating to clients and to personnel?

32. Am I prepared to make myself my "most important client?"

Chapter 10—Obtaining Clients

33. Have I assessed my selling skills and made arrangements to supplement or correct any deficiencies?

34. Can I list several hundred friends, acquaintances, and business and professional associates that would be interested in knowing that I started my own practice?

35. Have I put in writing my overall marketing strategy?

36. Have I considered how to acknowledge those people who refer business to me?

37. Does my marketing plan include the ability to track where my referrals come from?

38. Have I investigated both cost and results obtained by others using direct marketing techniques?

39. Do I have a plan to maintain contact with clients, client sources, and potential clients?

	Yes	No	N/A

40. Have I considered each of the many facets of projecting a professional image?

- Dress
- Physical presence
- Speech and expression
- Manners
- Office appearance
- Reports and correspondence
- Associated personnel
- Telephone image

41. Am I confident enough in my ability to sit face to face with a prospective client and sell my services?

42. Have I considered all aspects and possible repercussions of taking clients away from a former employer?

43. Have I given consideration to how to market my specialty?

Chapter 11—Managing Clients and Handling Fees

44. Have I designed engagement letters to use on the following?

- Audits
- Reviews
- Compilations
- Business tax returns
- Individual tax returns
- Special engagements

45. Because time in my own practice is, literally, money, have I an adequate structure set up for recording time and billing clients?

46. Have I determined my fee structure, and is it fair to me and my clients?

47. Do I know where to get information on setting a fee structure?

	Yes	No	N/A

48. Have I determined how I will bill for any specialized expertise? ___ ___ ___

49. If I choose to offer services on a fixed-fee basis for recurring work, have I made provisions for the following?

   • Monitoring the jobs ___ ___ ___

   • Limiting excessive demands ___ ___ ___

   • Periodic increases in fees ___ ___ ___

   • A clear understanding ___ ___ ___

Chapter 12—Billing and Collection Techniques

50. Have I determined how I will handle client billing issues, including situations that require a retainer? ___ ___ ___

51. Do I know how to use different methods to expedite billing and increase cash flow?

   • Detailed explanations of billing (to avoid client questions and confusion) ___ ___ ___

   • Payment at the time services are rendered ___ ___ ___

   • Interim billings ___ ___ ___

   • Use of credit cards ___ ___ ___

52. Have I formulated plans for how to deal with slow-paying clients, fee disputes, and compromise situations? ___ ___ ___

53. Do I have a policy on whether or not I will sue for a fee, and have I considered the many implications of this policy? ___ ___ ___

Chapter 13—Difficult Clients and Client Situations

54. Have I outlined a client screening process to help me avoid or eliminate difficult or undesirable clients? ___ ___ ___

55. Have I worked through a plan of action to help overcome fee resistance by potential clients? ___ ___ ___

	Yes	*No*	*N/A*

56. Do I have in mind the answers to give potential clients who might ask about the size of my firm and quality and scope of my services?

57. Have I considered how to handle practitioner or client–related mistakes?

58. If I have difficult or undesirable clients, will I be able to dismiss them?

Chapter 14—Planning for Growth

59. Have I made plans for my firm after the initial one or two years?

60. Do I understand the difference between quantitative and qualitative growth?

Chapter 15—Nurturing Your Professional and Personal Development

61. Have I a plan to maintain my professional and technical edge, despite the time constraints and rigors of my own practice?

62. Are professional involvement, quality continuing education, and other forms of personal and professional expression an integral part of my overall plan of action?

Engagement Letters

The engagement letters in this appendix are reproduced by permission from the AICPA *MAP Handbook*. They appear in the 1990 edition as the following exhibits:

- 204–4. Audit Services
- 204–5. Compilation of Financial Statements and Tax Services
- 204–6. Review of Financial Statements and Tax Services
- 204–7. MAS Engagement
- 204–8. Individual Tax Services

Engagement letters are the natural follow–through to the engagement proposal, once all parties agree upon the services to be rendered. Engagement letters help avoid misunderstandings with client and staff, clarify contractual obligations (including those related to fees and payment terms), reduce legal liability, and explain the client's responsibility.

Most important, engagement letters help the beginning practitioner plan an engagement, determine appropriate fees, and set out terms and conditions for payment. This form of agreement is strongly recommended for all beginning practitioners and for all clients.

Engagement Letter—Audit Services

SWIFT, MARCH & COMPANY
Certified Public Accountants

[*Date*]
Mr. Thomas Thorp, President
Anonymous Company, Inc.
Route 32
Nowhere, Anystate 00000

Dear Mr. Thorp:

This will confirm our understanding of the arrangements for our audit of the financial statements of Anonymous Company, Inc., for the year ending [*date*].

We will audit the Company's balance sheet at [*date*], and the related statements of income, retained earnings, and cash flows for the year then ended, for the purpose of expressing an opinion on them. The financial statements are the responsibility of the Company's management. Our responsibility is to express an opinion on the financial statements based on our audit.

We will conduct our audit in accordance with generally accepted auditing standards. Those standards require that we plan and perform the audit to obtain reasonable assurance about whether the financial statements are free of material misstatement. An audit includes examining, on a test basis, evidence supporting the amounts and disclosures in the financial statements. An audit also includes assessing the accounting principles used and significant estimates made by management, as well as evaluating the overall financial statement presentation. We believe that our audit will provide a reasonable basis for our opinion.

Our procedures will include tests of documentary evidence supporting the transactions recorded in the accounts, tests of the physical existence of inventories, and direct confirmation of receivables and certain other assets and liabilities by correspondence with selected customers, creditors, legal counsel, and banks. At the conclusion of our audit, we will request certain written representations from you about the financial statements and matters related thereto.

Our audit is subject to the inherent risk that material errors and irregularities, including fraud or defalcations, if they exist, will not be detected. However, we will inform you of irregularities that come to our attention, unless they are inconsequential.

If you intend to publish or otherwise reproduce the financial statements and make reference to our firm, you agree to provide us with printers' proofs or masters for our review and approval before printing. You also agree to provide us with a copy of the final reproduced material for our approval before it is distributed.

We will review the Company's federal and state [*identify states*] income tax returns for the fiscal year ended [*date*]. These returns, we understand, will be prepared by the controller.

Further, we will be available during the year to consult with you on the tax effects of any proposed transactions or contemplated changes in business policies.

Our fee for these services will be at our regular per diem rates, plus travel and other out–of–pocket costs. Invoices will be rendered every two weeks and are payable on presentation.

We are pleased to have this opportunity to serve you.

If this letter correctly expresses your understanding, please sign the enclosed copy where indicated and return it to us.*

Very truly yours,

SWIFT, MARCH & COMPANY

_____
Partner

APPROVED:

By_____

Date_____

_____

* Some accountants prefer not to obtain an acknowledgment, in which case their letter would omit the paragraph beginning "If this letter. . ." and the spaces for the acknowledgment. The first paragraph of their letter might begin as follows: "This letter sets forth our understanding of the terms and objectives of our audit. . . ."

Engagement Letter—Compilation of Financial Statements and Tax Services

SWIFT, MARCH & COMPANY
Certified Public Accountants

[*Date*]
Mr. Tom Jones, President
ZYXWV Freight Corporation
648 Crystal Lane
Noplace, Anystate 00000

Dear Mr. Jones:

This letter is to confirm our understanding of the terms and objectives of our engagement and the nature and limitations of the services we will provide.

We will perform the following services:

1. We will compile, from information you provide, the annual and interim balance sheets and related statements of income, retained earnings, and cash flows of ZYXWV Freight Corporation for the year 19XX. We will not audit or review such financial statements. Our report on the annual financial statements of ZYXWV Freight Corporation is presently expected to read as follows:

   > We have compiled the accompanying balance sheet ZYXWV Freight Corporation as of December 31, 19XX, and the related statements of income, retained earnings, and cash flows for the year then ended, in accordance with standards established by the American Institute of Certified Public Accountants.
   >
   > A compilation is limited to presenting in the form of financial statements information that is the representation of management (owners). We have not audited or reviewed the accompanying financial statements and, accordingly, do not express an opinion or any other form of assurance on them.

   Our report on your interim financial statements, which statements will omit substantially all disclosures, will include an additional paragraph that will read as follows:

   > Management has elected to omit substantially all of the disclosures required by generally accepted accounting principles. If the omitted disclosures were included in the financial statements, they might influence the user's conclusions about the Company's financial position, results of operations, and cash flows. Accordingly, these financial statements are not designed for those who are not informed about such matters.

If, for some reason, we are unable to complete the compilation of your financial statements, we will not issue a report on such statements as a result of this engagement.

2 . We will assist your bookkeeper in adjusting the books of account so that he will be able to prepare a working trial balance from which financial statements can be compiled. Your bookkeeper will provide us with a detailed trial balance and any supporting schedules we require.

3 . We will also prepare the federal and state [*identify states*] income tax returns for ZYXWV Freight Corporation for the fiscal year ended December 31, 19XX.

Our engagement cannot be relied upon to disclose errors and irregularities, including fraud or defalcations, that may exist. However, we will inform you of irregularities that come to our attention, unless they are inconsequential.

Our fee for these services will be at our regular per diem rates, plus travel and other out-of-pocket costs. Invoices will be rendered every two weeks and are payable on presentation.

We shall be pleased to discuss this letter with you at any time.

If the foregoing is in accordance with your understanding, please sign the copy of this letter in the space provided and return it to us.*

Sincerely yours,

_____

Swift, March & Company

Acknowledged:

ZYXWV Freight Corporation

_____

President

_____

Date

---

* Some accountants prefer not to obtain an acknowledgment, in which case their letter would omit the paragraph beginning "If the foregoing. . ." and the spaces for the acknowledgment. The first paragraph of their letter might begin as follows: "This letter sets forth our understanding of the terms and objectives of our engagement. . . ."

Engagement Letter—Review of Financial Statements and Tax Services

SWIFT, MARCH & COMPANY
Certified Public Accountants

[*Date*]
Mr. Tom Jones, President
ZYXWV Freight Company
648 Crystal Lane
Noplace, Anystate 00000

Dear Mr. Jones:

This letter is to confirm our understanding of the terms and objectives of our engagement and the nature and limitations of the services we will provide.

We will perform the following services:

1. We will review the balance sheet of ZYXWV Freight Company as of [*date*], and the related statements of income, retained earnings, and cash flows for the year then ended, in accordance with standards established by the American Institute of Certified Public Accountants. We will not perform an audit of such financial statements taken as a whole, and, accordingly, we do not express an opinion on them. A review does not contemplate obtaining an understanding of the internal control structure or assessing control risk, tests of accounting records and responses to inquiries by obtaining corroborating evidential matter, and certain other procedures ordinarily performed during an audit. Thus, a review does not provide assurance that we will become aware of all significant matters that would be disclosed in an audit. Our engagement cannot be relied upon to disclose errors, irregularities, or illegal acts, including fraud or defalcations, that may exist. However, we will inform you of any such matters that come to our attention, unless they are inconsequential.

Our report is presently expected to read as follows:

> We have reviewed the accompanying balance sheet of ZYXWV Freight Company as of [*date*], and the related statements of income, retained earnings, and cash flows for the year then ended, in accordance with standards established by the American Institute of Certified Public Accountants. All information included in these financial statements is the representation of the management of ZYXWV Freight Company.
>
> A review consists principally of inquiries of Company personnel and analytical procedures applied to financial data. It is substantially less in scope than an audit in accordance with generally

accepted auditing standards, the objective of which is the expression of an opinion regarding the financial statements taken as a whole. Accordingly, we do not express such an opinion.

Based on our review, we are not aware of any material modifications that should be made to the accompanying financial statements in order for them to be in conformity with generally accepted accounting principles.

If, for some reason, we are unable to complete our review of your financial statements, we will not issue a report on such statements as a result of this engagement.

2. We will provide your chief accountant with such consultation on accounting matters as he may require in adjusting and closing the books of account and in drafting financial statements for our review. Your chief accountant also will provide us with a detailed trial balance and any supporting schedules we require.

3. We will also prepare the federal and state [*identify states*] income tax returns for ZYXWV Freight Company for the fiscal year ended [*date*].

Our fee for these services will be at our regular per diem rates, plus travel and other out-of-pocket costs. Invoices will be rendered every two weeks and are payable on presentation.

We shall be pleased to discuss this letter with you at any time.

If the foregoing is in accordance with your understanding, please sign the copy of this letter in the space provided and return it to us.*

Sincerely yours,

_____

Swift, March & Company

Acknowledged:

ZYXWV Freight Corporation

_____

President

_____

Date

---

* Some accountants prefer not to obtain an acknowledgment, in which case their letter would omit the paragraph beginning "If the foregoing..." and the spaces for the acknowledgment. The first paragraph of their letter might begin as follows: "This letter sets forth our understanding of the terms and objectives of our engagement...."

Engagement Letter—MAS Engagement

SWIFT, MARCH & COMPANY
Certified Public Accountants

[*Date*]
Mr. Alexander Smith, Executive Director
Memorial Hospital
Youngstown, OH 00000

Dear Mr. Smith:

This letter confirms the services we discussed last week with you and your administrative staff about ways our firm might help Memorial Hospital achieve and maintain one of its major goals: progressive leadership in the community and the region in the delivery of quality health care services at a reasonable cost. In particular, we discussed potential operating efficiencies in systems, methods, and organization.

Problem Areas

Memorial Hospital's systems operate relatively smoothly and without major disruptions, but substantial improvements can be achieved in a number of areas.

Communications. Memorial, as do most hospitals, faces a continuing problem of maintaining the flow of essential, detailed information among its many departments, shifts, and specialties. Also, the hospital's responsibilities to the local medical practice, the patients, and the community require an elaborate and complex information network extending far beyond the hospital.

Because of its complexity, this network frequently fails to provide essential, timely information. As a result, extra work loads tend to be created throughout the hospital.

Closing the gaps in this network will eliminate the extra work loads and unnecessary associated risks and will result in more reliable and efficient internal operation.

Paper Work. Again, in common with other hospitals, Memorial faces massive paper work requirements. From internal accounting records and insurance forms to medical records and charts, the total recordkeeping is a major portion of Memorial's work load, perhaps equaling direct patient care in man hours and labor costs.

A concentrated effort to streamline this paper work could save much time and money in almost every hospital function.

Organization, Staffing, and Work Assignments. As the cost of services has increased, the traditional methods of organizing and operating a modern hospital have come under close scrutiny from administrators, insurance departments, legislators, and the public.

Hospitals must reexamine their methods and restructure their activities for higher efficiency and economy than was expected in past years.

Aside from the economics of this problem, Memorial Hospital has grown to a point where this type of reexamination is essential to maintain leadership among the area hospitals.

Operations Improvement Program

Working closely with hospital personnel, we will make a careful and comprehensive review of the full range of your activities—from Nursing Services and ancillary departments, to Administration, Maintenance, and Housekeeping—to identify and evaluate:

- Formal and informal organization structures
- Paperwork systems and procedures
- Current work assignments
- Staffing and staff utilization
- Supervisory, managerial, and administrative requirements
- Communications network and information requirements, including management reports
- Facilities scheduling methods

We will extensively interview administrators, department heads, supervisors, and selected staff members, as well as members of key medical staff committees. You have assured us of their full cooperation. We will also examine in detail all currently used forms and documents, and thoroughly analyze reports and records covering hospital operations. In our review, we will consider Memorial Hospital's near-term growth and expansion.

After we review and evaluate each area listed above, we will prepare two types of detailed recommendations for operational improvements:

- Those that can be implemented rapidly (without extensive system design or conversion efforts)
- Those that require a system design and implementation project to install

Each recommended change will be supported by an analysis of projected benefits—increased efficiency, improved communications, and prospective cost reductions. Each change will also show a proposed implementation schedule.

We consider this integrated program the most economic and effective approach to Memorial Hospital's objectives.

Expected Benefits

A project of this type can be expected to yield the following:

Recommendations for Rapid Improvements

- Modify the existing communications network to materially improve communications and response. For the short term, we would expect to close major communications gaps and eliminate major redundancies.
- Reduce paper work volume through consolidation of forms and minor form modifications, and eliminate unnecessary paper work.
- Improve operational efficiency through limited adjustments of work loads and work assignments.

Our experience with similar projects has shown 1% to 2% payroll reduction arising directly from these types of recommendations. From this experience and our preliminary review of your hospital operations, we estimate a potential annual cost reduction of more than $50,000 without impairing operational efficiency.

Implementation Projects. Until the detailed review is complete, we are not prepared to identify the prospective benefits of major recommendations, although our experience is that substantial additional improvement will result.

In presenting each major recommendation, we will clearly identify the specific benefits, the expected cost to implement, and the proposed plan. Thus, Memorial Hospital will be able to judge the value and priority of each project before proceeding with it.

Project Organization

The project will be under the overall supervision of a partner from our firm's MAS division, who will work closely with Mr. Schlag. The staff will consist of a supervisory consultant, a senior consultant, a team of four analysts, and one or two hospital employees assigned full-time to our analyst staff.

We also ask that the hospital assign part-time liaison representatives from the nursing and medical staffs to provide technical support in those areas.

Fee Estimate and Timetable

We estimate that our fee for this project will range from $40,000 to $44,000. Our policy is to bill every two weeks for services and costs. Payment is due when invoices are rendered.

We will keep you informed of our progress during the engagement. If time actually spent is less than our estimate, you will be billed for the lesser amount. If we encounter extraordinary problems that could increase the quoted fee, we will inform you immediately. You have agreed to pay us a $27,500 retainer to apply against the final billing.

We are pleased to have you as a client and hope this will begin a long and pleasant association.

If the above agrees with your understanding of the terms of our engagement, please sign the copy of this letter in the space provided and return it to us together with a check for $27,500.

Very truly yours,

SWIFT, MARCH & COMPANY

_____
Partner

RESPONSE:

This letter correctly sets forth the understanding of Memorial Hospital.

Officer signature: _____

Title: _____

Date: _____

Engagement Letter—Individual Tax Services

Dear Client:

We appreciate the opportunity of working with you and advising you regarding your income tax. To ensure a complete understanding between us, we are setting forth the pertinent information about the services which we propose to render for you.

We will prepare your 19XX federal and requested state income tax returns from information which you will furnish to us. We will make no audit or other verification of the data you submit, although we may need to ask you for clarification of some of the information. We will furnish you with questionnaires and/or worksheets to guide you in gathering the necessary information for us. Your use of such forms will assist us in keeping our fee to a minimum.

The law provides for a penalty to be imposed where a taxpayer makes a substantial understatement of their tax liability. If you would like information on the amount or circumstances of this penalty, please let us know.

You have the final responsibility for the income tax returns and, therefore, you should review them carefully before you sign and file them.

Our work in connection with the preparation of your income tax returns does not include any procedures designed to discover defalcations or other irregularities, should any exist. We will render such accounting and bookkeeping assistance as we find necessary for preparation of the income tax returns.

We will use our judgment in resolving questions where the tax law is unclear, or where there may be conflicts between the taxing authorities' interpretations of the law and other supportable positions. Unless otherwise instructed by you, we will resolve such questions in your favor whenever possible.

Our fee for these services will be based upon the amount of time required at our standard billing rates, plus out-of-pocket expenses. All invoices are due and payable upon presentation.

Your returns may be selected for review by the taxing authorities. Any proposed adjustments by the examining agent are subject to certain rights of appeal. In the event of such government tax examination, we will be available upon request to represent you and will render additional invoices for the time and expenses incurred.

If the foregoing fairly sets forth your understanding, please sign this letter in the space indicated and return it to our office.

We want to express our appreciation for this opportunity to work with you.

Very truly yours,

Accepted by: _____

Date: _____

Sample Business Plan and Loan Proposal

The business plan and loan proposal has a double purpose: to give the CPA a clear, strategic vision for directing day-to-day operations and to assist in obtaining financing. This appendix briefly outlines the steps in preparing a business plan and loan proposal and also includes an example of a plan and proposal.

The Business Plan

The first step in creating a business plan is to identify your business and determine its unique characteristics. This "uniqueness" is something that makes your firm thrive or something you offer that others do not. It might be an ability to solve problems in an unusual and creative fashion, a budding specialization, or an exceptional business location. Whatever that particular plus factor is, it should be the central theme around which you build and advertise your practice.

Once you establish the key characteristics you want to emphasize in your business plan, you are ready to write the introduction. The introduction should outline the key elements of your business plan and stimulate the reader's interest in your concept and plan of action.

In your introduction, touch on the following eight key issues:

1. The business you are in
2. The services you will offer
3. The firm's unique strength
4. The management team's experience
5. The growth potential of the business
6. How much money you need
7. How you will use the money
8. How the bank achieves a return and secures its loan

Following the introduction, you should provide a one- or two-page summary on management and organization. This is crucial for a beginning practitioner. It is where you must convince the lender you have the experience and background necessary to manage your business and safeguard the investment in your firm. Although you can touch on your technical skills, concentrate on managerial skills and achievements. Keep in mind the plan is as much for the benefit of the owners as it is for the lender.

After discussing management and organization, include several descriptive pages on marketing. Essential elements to cover include the general market availability pertinent to your anticipated services, the competition, your specific marketing plan (including any target market), and your anticipated results.

Next, address the firm's operations. This is particularly important to CPAs. Bankers usually have a high regard for a CPA's creditworthiness and technical skills. However, not all CPAs know how to run a practice; remember the third "C" of credit is capacity—a person's ability to manage a business. Therefore, in this section of your business plan, you need to convince the banker that you have a well-thought-out plan for your business. Cover such things as efforts preparatory to starting your firm; the planned operation, including staffing and facilities; and, finally, provisions for a review process and other forms of backup or professional support.

The last part of the business plan features the financial plan. The amount of information provided is up to you. At a minimum, give a forecasted operating statement for three to five years, use of loan proceeds and cash position during the period, and forecasted balance sheets. Adequate explanation of all of the underlying assumptions and rationale is also recommended.

When preparing your statement of forecasted operations, you might want to consider the following suggestions.

1. *Project services.* It is difficult to project services. Typically, when based on known contacts, numbers will be too modest. In addition, it is difficult to quantify marketing efforts. To estimate your projected services, I suggest you use a survey of established practitioners. For example, the Texas Society's *National Report—Practice Management Survey—1989* contains operating results of nearly 1,700 sole practitioners. The 1989 survey indicated that average net fees were $166,000 for sole practitioners. It might not be unreasonable, therefore, to project that in your first year you will generate 30 to 40 percent of what the average would do.

2. *Employ logic.* Approach your financial projections from several directions. Assume that you project one–third of the average, or

approximately $55,000. Do you have the hours available to generate the fees? If you anticipate you will have 1,000 client hours available and you expect a net rate of $50 to $60 per hour, your ability to generate the projected returns is logical. If, however, you project two–thirds of the average, or approximately $100,000, with the same client–hour availability, your projections are unreasonable.

Other factors should also be considered. If you have a base of clients to start with, say $10,000, then it is easier to project $40,000 or $50,000 in services. Also, if you have a specialty that draws premium rates over conventional services, it will be easier to project more in services.

3. *Create a backup plan.* Your financial plan should be flexible. Allow for some contingencies; if clients are not procured at the projected pace, you can always teach or perform contract services for other CPAs in order to meet your financial needs and goals, although if you do, you delay obtaining your long–term financial objectives.

4. *Be objective.* The last person you should deceive is yourself. You have to be convinced that the plan you created makes sense. Similarly, your banker must be persuaded that your plan is viable. Be objective in your forecasts and projections.

5. *Be prepared to risk.* As mentioned in chapter 7, "Financing Your Business," you may have to place personal assets as collateral for your business loan. Common collateral is a second mortgage on your residence and, possibly, cash value of insurance or securities. If you are unwilling to place personal assets at risk, you may want to rethink your decision to go solo.

If the bank you approach does not have a personal financial statement on file, then you will probably need to furnish one as part of or adjunct to your business plan.

The following section contains a sample Business Plan and Loan Proposal for a starting sole practitioner. The information is hypothetical but approximates the data that might be contained in a plan and proposal.

JANE L. JENSON, CPA
BUSINESS PLAN AND LOAN PROPOSAL

Prepared for

First National Bank

October 1, 1990

Table of Contents

Introduction

Management and Organization

Marketing

Operations

Financial Plan and Related Information

Pro Forma Financial Statements

Introduction

The certified public accounting firm of Jane L. Jenson is to be formally established on November 1, 1990. The principal of the firm, Jane L. Jenson, is an experienced practitioner with over seven years of public accounting experience with both local and international firms. She also has experience in diverse industries and an extensive background in several tax specializations.

Ms. Jenson was a manager in the tax department of Abbott, Norman and Company, Certified Public Accountants, prior to leaving to establish her own practice. At the firm, she was primarily responsible for foreign taxation and employee benefit programs. Ms. Jenson plans to continue those specialties in her own practice.

As noted in the marketing section of this proposal, the firm will capitalize on Ms. Jenson's academic training and specialized practice experience. The marketing plan also projects a considerable effort directed toward general tax service currently being requested of CPAs.

Though the firm is being established initially as a sole proprietorship, growth and expansion plans are already in the formulative stages (see section on operations), as a result of office-sharing and exchange of service arrangements.

The business plan and loan proposal projects a business loan of $30,000. The loan will be in two parts, the first of which is $10,000 for equipment, furnishings, and initial promotional efforts. That loan is to be amortized monthly for four years and collateralized by initial and hereinafter-acquired equipment and furnishings. The balance, $20,000, is to be a revolving line of credit collateralized by all other assets of the firm, including accounts receivable and necessary personal assets held outside the firm.

Management and Organization

Jane L. Jenson graduated from Central State University with a B.S. in Business Administration. She earned a Master of Taxation degree in 1981 from the same school, while employed at an international accounting firm.

During a total of over seven years of public accounting with two different firms, she has—

- Attended various staff-level training programs.
- Attended a total of twenty-eight formal continuing education seminars and conferences on various tax, accounting, and practice management topics.
- Achieved all designated supervisory positions on or before targeted time frame.
- Held the position of senior staff person in both foreign and employee benefit taxation at the time she left her most recent employment, a twenty-five-person, two-office firm.
- Had client responsibilities in various industries and professions. This included extensive client interaction, tax planning, client billing, and problem resolution. She has also represented clients before the Internal Revenue Service.
- Had three staff subordinates assigned to her, along with varied administrative and temporary tax-season personnel in her capacity as a Tax Manager at Abbott, Norman and Company. In 1986 she received the firm's Employee of the Year Award for outstanding contribution to the firm.

Ms. Jenson will locate her offices in Suite 350, Harrison Towers building. She will share offices with a two-partner CPA firm, Burns and Overstreet, CPAs. Burns and Overstreet has administrative and technical staff support available, as well as other office amenities and support needs such as library facilities, reproduction equipment, and computers.

Ms. Jenson has also arranged for additional technical support and review from her former employer.

Marketing

Ms. Jenson will offer two primary services: conventional tax services and two specialized services, foreign taxation and pension and profit sharing.

The conventional services, while not unique, are unquestionably in much demand in the metropolitan area. Recent major tax legislation and ongoing revision of tax laws have created opportunities for a number of recently opened competent accounting firms. Additionally, long-established accounting firms in the area continue to grow each year. According to a survey of over 350 accounting firms in the state, the average growth in services in the last three years is in excess of 16 percent annually.

Further evidence of the demand for competent tax services is the continual search by established firms for experienced (three years or more) accountants to work in tax compliance.

The available market for CPAs' conventional tax services is presently divided among three international accounting firms, sixteen regional and large local accounting firms, and approximately 250 small firms, including sole practitioners like Ms. Jenson. A number of tax practitioners, enrolled agents, and other noncertified individuals compete in tax compliance. However, those practitioners and their clients are not considered part of the CPA market, although there is some overlap.

Ms. Jenson's office location is in the metropolitan area's Northwest quadrant and is specifically located in the recently developed Airport Industrial Park, a development of nearly eighty acres of commercial and industrial facilities. Some studies project this development to be the anchor of future development projects, particularly if contracts are let for the expansion of the airport.

At the present time, only a modest number of CPA firms are located in the area, although more will likely locate there in the future as the new office complexes are completed.

This location was selected as a complement to one of Ms. Jenson's specialties—foreign taxation. The Airport Industrial Park contains twenty-three businesses involved to some degree in importing and exporting products to the Far East. A number of the businesses have branch offices in Hong Kong, Tokyo, and Seoul. Even though most of those businesses are currently being served by other CPA firms, there are significant possibilities of either consulting projects with other CPAs or actual client acquisition.

Ms. Jenson's specific marketing program includes—

- Mailing of announcements to approximately 250 individuals and firms with whom there exists a personal, business, or client relationship.

- Becoming involved in or expanding activities in three civic/community groups: the Airport Industrial Park Business Association, the Lake Valley Optimist Club, and the Greater Metropolitan Estate Planning Council. She will also continue professional activities in the State Society of CPAs and the American Institute of Certified Public Accountants.

- She will develop and offer three seminars to interested parties on "Tax Advantages to Developing New Markets in the Far East," "Can You Sell 'Made in the USA' to the Far Eastern Market?" and "Fringe Benefits for Your Employees and the Related Advantage to You."

These seminars will be offered on a no-charge basis to interested individuals or firms. The mailings for the seminars will concentrate on bankers, firms in the Airport Industrial Park area, and new businesses.

- Ms. Jenson will also utilize a preprinted tax newsletter of general interest for clients, prospective clients, and other interested parties. She will prepare and distribute quarterly a newsletter dealing exclusively with foreign taxation for clients and other CPAs in the community.

The above marketing plan should result in an estimated $20,000 to $40,000 in general tax services the first twelve months and $20,000 to $40,000 in specialized services in from six to eighteen months. The second specialty is estimated to generate from $10,000 to $20,000 in services, primarily from other CPAs.

The above marketing results, when coupled with the existing base of clientele, will attain the approximate results projected under the financial plan. If the marketing effort does not result in clients as projected, the following alternative efforts can be implemented:

- Accelerate the effort to obtain conventional services through direct mail and yellow page advertising. The direct mail campaign will be in concert with seminars, public speaking, and writing tax articles for area newspapers.

- Increase the number of hours available for contract or per-diem work for two other CPA firms.

The long-range marketing plan, after 1991, contemplates a significant concentration in foreign taxation, assuming a continued interest in those markets by local business entities. The foundation for that marketing effort will be laid in the next two years by expanding professional contact with other CPAs and professional activities, as well as the seminars and newsletters previously noted.

Additional marketing efforts will include writing articles for national publications, service with industry trade organizations, and target marketing of businesses in the Far East market sector.

Operations

In anticipation of starting her own firm, Ms. Jenson began an accelerated program of study on managing an accounting practice in 1987. This program included extensive research on the topic through self-study courses, professional reading, and several seminars and conferences. She spent over forty hours in reviewing several other firms' operations, including, with permission, her former employer, Abbott, Norman and Company. Her present reference library includes various authorities on successful practice management.

Her practice will be part of an office-sharing arrangement with two former coworkers at an international accounting firm. These individuals, Larry Burns and Paul Overstreet, established their own firm three years ago. They recently leased approximately 2,000 feet of office space in the Harrison Towers building, located in the Airport Industrial Park complex. Ms. Jenson will sublease one office and have access to a conference room, storage, and kitchen facilities. She will also share administrative staff and other necessary support such as library facilities.

Burns and Overstreet currently employ one CPA, one paraprofessional accountant, and a secretary. They have agreed to utilize Ms. Jenson for tax work overload, her schedule permitting. There is a preliminary agreement that Ms. Jenson will refer accounting and auditing work to them, and they will refer foreign tax and complex employee benefit tax work to her.

There has also been some preliminary discussion about future growth and association between the entities. Both parties agreed to defer detailed discussion until after Ms. Jenson's firm is fully established.

The advantage to this arrangement is that it allows for an economy of expenditure, an ability to market all usual services offered by a CPA, a review process, and staff assistants when needed.

Financial Plan and Related Information

The borrower will furnish quarterly financial statements on the business operation. The borrower will also furnish personal financial statements if and as required by the bank.

The following financial information is attached.

- *Forecasted Balance Sheets.* Balance sheets at November 30, 1990, December 31, 1990, 1991, and 1992, are presented, reflecting the results of operations, initial capitalization, and loan activity.

- *Statements of Forecasted Operations.* This statement reflects a best estimate of projected operations for the months of November and December 1990, and years ended December 31, 1991 and 1992.

- *Statements of Forecasted Cash Flows.* This statement reflects the cash position of the firm after respective operating periods ended November and December 1990, and December 1991 and 1992. It also includes a Reconciliation of Net Income to Net Cash Provided (Used) by Operating Activities.

- *Summary of Significant Forecast Assumptions and Accounting Policies.* Disclosure related to the assumption and policies used, along with explanatory details or schedules follow the three noted financial statements.

I have compiled the accompanying forecasted balance sheets, statements of income, and cash flows of Jane L. Jenson, CPA, as of November 30, and December 31, 1990, and December 31, 1991, and 1992, and for the respective periods then ending, in accordance with standards established by the American Institute of Certified Public Accountants.

A compilation is limited to presenting in the form of a forecast information that is the representation of management and does not include evaluation of the support for the assumptions underlying the forecast. I have not examined the forecast and, accordingly, do not express an opinion or any other form of assurance on the accompanying statements or assumptions. Furthermore, there will usually be differences between the forecasted and actual results, because events and circumstances frequently do not occur as expected, and those differences may be material. I have no responsibility to update this report for events and circumstances occurring after the date of this report.

I am not independent with respect to Jane L. Jenson, CPA.

Certified Public Accountant
October 1, 1990

JANE L. JENSON, CPA

Forecasted Balance Sheets

	November 30, 1990	December 31, 1990	December 31, 1991	December 31, 1992
Assets				
Current assets:				
Cash	$ 6,700	$ 2,800	$ 3,100	$ 4,900
Billed receivables		3,000	12,600	26,600
Noncurrent assets:				
Furniture and equipment	7,500	7,300	4,900	2,500
	$14,200	$13,100	$20,600	$34,000
Liabilities				
Current liabilities:				
Bank loans:				
Term	$10,000	$ 9,800	$ 7,400	$ 5,000
Revolving	—	—	15,000	10,000
Equity				
Jenson, Equity:				
Capital account	10,000	10,000	3,300	(1,800)
Operations	(5,800)	(5,700)	12,900	50,800
Withdrawals	—	(1,000)	(18,000)	(30,000)
	4,200	3,300	(1,800)	19,000
	$14,200	$13,100	$20,600	$34,000

See summary of significant forecast assumptions and accounting policies and accountant's report.

JANE L. JENSON, CPA

Statements of Forecasted Operations

	One Month Ended		One Year Ended	
	November 30, 1990	December 31, 1990	December 31, 1991	December 31, 1992
Revenues				
Services	—	$3,000	$60,000	$120,000
Expenses				
Office-sharing costs	$ 750	750	9,000	10,800
Administrative staff	—	—	6,000	18,000
Contract services	—	—	5,000	10,000
Malpractice insurance	250	250	3,000	5,000
Liability insurance	50	50	600	600
Office supplies	1,000	300	3,600	4,200
Library and publications	500	250	3,000	3,600
Professional activities	500	250	3,000	3,000
Marketing	2,500	500	6,000	6,000
Automobile	250	250	3,000	3,600
Depreciation	—	200	2,400	2,400
Interest	—	100	2,500	2,000
	5,800	2,900	47,100	69,200
Net Income (Loss)	$(5,800)	$ 100	$12,900	$ 50,800

See summary of significant forecast assumptions and accounting policies and accountant's report.

JANE L. JENSON, CPA

Statements of Forecasted Cash Flows

	One Month Ended		One Year Ended	
	November 30, 1990	December 31, 1990	December 31, 1991	December 31, 1992
Cash Flows From Operating Activities				
Cash received from clients			$50,400	$106,000
Cash paid to suppliers and employees	$(5,800)	$(2,600)	(42,200)	(64,800)
Interest paid		(100)	(2,500)	(2,000)
Net cash provided (used) by operations activities	(5,800)	(2,700)	5,700	39,200
Cash Flows From Investing Activities				
Capital expenditures	(7,500)			
Cash Flows From Financing Activities				
Net borrowings under lines of credit			15,000	(5,000)
Term loan proceeds	10,000			
Principal payments on term loan		(200)	(2,400)	(2,400)
Initial owner's equity contribution	10,000			
Owner's withdrawals		(1,000)	(18,000)	(30,000)
Net cash provided (used) by financing activities	20,000	(1,200)	(5,400)	(37,400)
Net increase (decrease) in cash	6,700	(3,900)	300	1,800
Cash at Beginning of Period		6,700	2,800	3,100
Cash at End of Period	$ 6,700	$ 2,800	$ 3,100	$ 4,900

See summary of significant forecast assumptions and accounting policies and accountant's report.

JANE L. JENSON, CPA

Statements of Forecasted Cash Flows (cont.)

	One Month Ended		One Year Ended	
	November 30, 1990	*December 31, 1990*	*December 31, 1991*	*December 31, 1992*
Reconciliation of Net Income to Net Cash Provided (Used) by Operating Activities:				
Net (Loss) Income	$(5,800)	$ 100	$12,900	$50,800
Adjustments to Reconcile Net Income to Net Cash Provided				
Depreciation		200	2,400	2,400
Change in Assets and Liabilities				
Increase in billed receivables		(3,000)	(9,600)	(14,000)
Total adjustments		(2,800)	(7,200)	(11,600)
Net Cash Provided (Used) by Operating Activities	$(5,800)	$(2,700)	$(5,700)	$(39,200)

JANE L. JENSON, CPA

Summary of Significant Forecast Assumptions
and Accounting Policies

Note A. Nature of the Forecasts
This financial forecast presents, to the best of management's knowledge
and belief, the Firm's expected financial position, results of operations,
and cash flows for the forecast period. Accordingly, the forecast reflects
its judgment as of October 1, 1990, the date of this forecast, of the
expected conditions and the Firm's expected course of action. There
usually will be differences between the forecasted and actual results,
because events and circumstances frequently do not occur as expected,
and those differences may be material.

Note B. Nature of Operations During the Forecast Period
The forecast financial data accompanies a business plan of Jane L. Jenson,
CPA, which describes the nature of the Firm's operation.

Note C. Revenues
The revenue projections are based on the following assumptions:

	Year Ended December 31,	
	1991	*1992*
General tax services	$30,000	$ 60,000
Foreign tax specialty	15,000	30,000
Pension plan services	10,000	20,000
Other	5,000	10,000
	$60,000	$120,000

In the first full year of operation, the projection reflects approximately
one-third of the volume experienced by average sole practitioners
according to a survey by the Texas Society of CPAs of approximately
1,700 CPAs throughout the country.

Though the above figures are estimates, the firm does have commitments for approximately $12,500 in work during the first quarter, 1991.
See the comments under the marketing portion of the business plan.

Note D. Furniture and Equipment
The initial furniture and equipment includes a computer and printer,
personal office furnishings, and selected small office equipment. Most
major furniture and equipment is provided through an office-sharing
affiliation.

Note E. Financing

The Firm contemplates $30,000 in available financing after initial capitalization of $10,000 by Jane L. Jenson. A $10,000 term loan will be utilized to acquire initial furnishings and equipment and to fund initial marketing efforts. A line of credit will be utilized to a projected $20,000 in summer 1991, with a fall repayment of $5,000 in the same year and an additional similar reduction in 1992.

Note F. Owner's Withdrawals

The owner anticipates withdrawals as follows:

First month of operation	—
December 1990	$1,000
Year 1990—monthly	1,500
Year 1992—monthly	2,500

There are limited personal contingency funds available to the owner, in the event the operation does not generate necessary cash flows.

Note G. Expenses

The following summarizes significant assumptions for forecasted expenses.

1. Expenses will generally be paid in the month incurred. Accordingly, no accounts payable are reflected.

2. Office-sharing arrangements have been negotiated with another CPA firm. The monthly costs will be $750 through December 31, 1991, and $900 per month through the year ended December 31, 1992. The shared services include one individual office, common reception areas, telephone answering, general tax library services, a minimum block of reproduction copies, and a minimum block of secretarial time.

3. It is anticipated administrative staff will be hired on a part-time basis in August 1991 and convert to full-time in 1992. Taxes and benefits are included in the figures listed.

4. Library and publications include the cost of texts and other reference material related to certain tax specialties of Jane L. Jenson.

5. Both office supplies and marketing have a disproportionate relationship in the initial month, November 1990, because both include initial acquisition and marketing efforts.

FAST-PLUS Exercise

This is a relatively fast tool for analyzing a potential public accounting partnership structure. It is designed to identify problems that might arise in the future.

Each potential partner should grade or rate the other in the various items noted. Whether or not they exchange the analyses with each other is a personal decision. Remember that criticism or what might be construed as criticism could hurt the relationship before it starts. However, *the primary purpose of the analysis is for each partner to assess his or her own feelings about the relationship.*

FAST-PLUS is an acronym for *Financial, Attributes and Attitudes, Spouses, and Technical Skills* concerns, plus a final question of some importance.

Instructions: Rate or grade your potential partner(s) or existing partner(s) on the following scale of 1 to 9, with one being the lowest rating and nine the highest.

    1, 2, 3: Below average (known problems)
    4, 5, 6: Average (potential problems)
    7, 8, 9: Above average (no serious problems)

There are also categories for "unknown" and "not applicable."

To give you a perspective: 1–3 could likely lead to a serious problem in the future, if not corrected; 4–6 rate acceptable situations that you would desire to have corrected but would not necessarily be seriously detrimental to the partnership; 7–9 characterize items that contribute considerably to a successful relationship.

FAST-PLUS

	1 2 3	4 5 6	7 8 9	N/K *	N/A †
Financial					
Parity of financial commitment	___	___	___	___	___
Personal financial situation	___	___	___	___	___
Working spouse	___	___	___	___	___
Spending habits	___	___	___	___	___
Attributes and Attitudes					
Commitment to work	___	___	___	___	___
Plans and goals for growth	___	___	___	___	___
Generates profits	___	___	___	___	___
Outside activities	___	___	___	___	___
Pleasing personality	___	___	___	___	___
Attitude towards staff	___	___	___	___	___
Attitude towards IRS	___	___	___	___	___
Honesty	___	___	___	___	___
Health	___	___	___	___	___
Personal goals	___	___	___	___	___
Relationship with other partners	___	___	___	___	___
Professional	___	___	___	___	___
Dress and appearance	___	___	___	___	___
Attitudes towards the partnership	___	___	___	___	___
Attitudes towards the future	___	___	___	___	___
Confidence	___	___	___	___	___
Delegates tasks appropriately	___	___	___	___	___

---

* Not known.
† Not applicable.

FAST-PLUS

	1 2 3	4 5 6	7 8 9	N/K*	N/A†
Attributes and Attitudes					
Personal habits	———	———	———	———	———
Morals	———	———	———	———	———
Spouse					
Influence	———	———	———	———	———
Attitude	———	———	———	———	———
Supportive	———	———	———	———	———
Financial dependence	———	———	———	———	———
Hours	———	———	———	———	———
Health	———	———	———	———	———
Children	———	———	———	———	———
Family activities	———	———	———	———	———
Other	———	———	———	———	———
Technical Skills					
Auditing—general	———	———	———	———	———
Profit	———	———	———	———	———
Not-for-profit	———	———	———	———	———
Tax—individual	———	———	———	———	———
Partnership	———	———	———	———	———
Corporation	———	———	———	———	———
Retirement	———	———	———	———	———
Planning	———	———	———	———	———
Audits	———	———	———	———	———
Estates and trusts	———	———	———	———	———
Other	———	———	———	———	———
Accounting—speed	———	———	———	———	———
Accuracy	———	———	———	———	———
Persistence	———	———	———	———	———
Knowledge	———	———	———	———	———
Computers					
General knowledge	———	———	———	———	———
Specific knowledge	———	———	———	———	———

---

* Not known.

† Not applicable.

FAST-PLUS (cont.)

Technical Skills	1 2 3	4 5 6	7 8 9	N/K*	N/A†
Practice management					
Client development	_____	_____	_____	_____	_____
Administration	_____	_____	_____	_____	_____
Personnel	_____	_____	_____	_____	_____
Other expertise	_____	_____	_____	_____	_____
General business acumen	_____	_____	_____	_____	_____
Overall complement of technical skills to other partners	_____	_____	_____	_____	_____
CPA exam	_____	_____	_____	_____	_____
Financial management	_____	_____	_____	_____	_____

Finally, you will note we have only indicated a rating up to "9." There was a purpose in this, and it was not to suggest there could *never* be a "10" partnership situation. It does suggest, however, that there are few perfect partnerships, much the same as there are few perfect marriages. We are suggesting you enter the relationship knowing there might be some potential problems ahead.

As a final test, the "Plus" portion of the exercise comments on your potential partner(s) or existing partner(s) as follows: List any situation you can think of that your partner might encounter for which you would not be *proud* to say, "This is *my* partner."

Social situation _____

_____

Client situation _____

_____

Professional situation _____

_____

Personal _____

_____

Other _____

_____

_____

_____

* Not known.
† Not applicable.

Summary

If you were not realistic when you assessed the foregoing, your time has not been well spent, because you will draw conclusions that will likely have a negative impact in the future. However, assume you were truthful and, further, assume there were some negative answers. This does not mean the association cannot work. It simply means there is at least one potential problem that must be resolved. Solving the problem can be handled in several ways: removing the problem or compensating for it. It is not likely that the problem can be solved by ignoring it.

A preponderance of rankings of 1–4 would obviously indicate a narrow chance of survival of the partnership. As a matter of fact, any category rated 4 or less should be closely scrutinized. Certain categories are more critical than others; for example, a 2 or 3 in "parity of financial commitment" is potentially more detrimental than, say, a 1 in one of the technical skills.

If the bulk of ratings range from 4 to 7 or 8, you have a good chance of success. All 8s and 9s are frosting on the cake.

With respect to the last factor (being proud to say, "This is *my* partner"), you need to be realistic. There can certainly be situations when you might not be proud. That does not necessarily mean you will not make a good association with the intended partner.

Associating with another CPA is a major step in development of a practice. Premature association can certainly hurt growth plans, as can the wrong selection. It is a step that should be taken only after careful consideration of the various factors that will affect much of your future professional (and, in some cases, personal) life.

Client Evaluation Questionnaire

CONFIDENTIAL

Client _____ Account Manager/Partner _____

Date _____

(Circle only one number in each group.)

What is usual condition of client's records?
2 Unusable or always late
4 Scattered but workable
6 Client needs orientation
8 Good
10 Excellent

What is client's potential growth?
5 Terminating
10 Decreasing
15 Level
20 Growing
25 Unlimited

What is client's attitude toward IRS?
1 Apprehensive
2 Hostile
5 Apathetic
8 Cooperative

What work is done for client?
3 Bookkeeping
6 Reviews or compilations
9 Audits
12 Year-end work and special services
15 Comprehensive services

Does client pay fees on time?
1 May never pay
2 Always 90 days late
5 Pays within 45 days
10 Pays when billed

How does client react to fees?
1 Fees always challenged as too high
5 Requires itemized bill
10 Usually accepts amount of bill
15 Wants service and expects to pay
20 Thinks we are superior—pays premium

What is the total annual fee?
3 To $1,500
6 $1,500–$5,000
9 $5,000–$10,000
12 Above $10,000

What is client's attitude toward recommending us?
1 Would never do so
2 Might do so
12 Has not recently
16 Does at times
20 Does frequently

What does client want from us?
1 Minimum service
2 Security regarding IRS
3 Counseling
4 Timely service
5 Direction and tax planning

From whom does client seek information?
1 Client's employees
2 News media
3 Client's competitors
4 Client's friends
5 Professionals (including us)

What is client's attitude toward his expenses?
1 Spendthrift
2 Niggardly
3 Economical
4 Liberal
5 Goes "first class"

Does client expose us to legal action?
1 High risk
2 Would consider suit
3 Low risk
4 Little risk
5 Would never sue

What is client's attitude toward our staff?
1 Critical and argumentative
2 Uncooperative
3 Usually cooperative
4 Businesslike
5 Friendly and appreciative

What is client's financial strength?
1 Insolvent
4 Solvent but undercapitalized
8 Adequate
10 Strong capital structure

Above conditions prevailed at month of _____

Evaluation by _____

Scoring:
  Maximum = 154 points
  Minimum = 23 points
  30 points and below = Drop client
  30 to 50 points = Evaluate in 90 days (on trial)
  50 to 70 points = Make an attempt to upgrade client
  70 points and above = Retain client

Total points _____

Make additional comments on back.

SOURCE: AICPA, *MAP Handbook,* rev. ed. (New York: AICPA, 1990), 204:39–40.

Lease Checklist

This checklist reflects matters to be considered when leasing office facilities. It also provides space to accumulate estimated costs.

The Form of the Lease and Its Terms

1. Designation of lessee (legal firm name).
2. Total annual rent.
3. Occupancy date.
4. Total floor space:
   a. "rentable" area (often includes hallways, lobbies, lavatories and common areas);
   b. "usable" area.
5. Initial term of lease.
6. Renewal term of lease (require notification by certified mail six months prior to lease expiration) and renewal rates.
7. Basis for passing through operating costs and real estate tax increases (escalation clauses).
8. Base year on which increases are to be computed.
9. Holding-over terms.
10. Expansion options (include right-of-first-refusal provision) and rental rates on expansion.
11. Required deposits (prepaid rent, security, etc.)
12. Provision for specific penalties for early termination.
13. Services furnished by landlord (e.g., security, HVAC, cleaning, electricity, etc.), or the estimated annual cost if not furnished. (Be sure that all services will be provided during off-hours, weekends and holidays as needed. Any restrictions should be noted in the lease.)
14. Terms of shared operating costs. (Is the policy fair? For instance, a health club or restaurant may be a tenant. They are likely to use more hot water and gas than a CPA firm.)
15. Penalty provision if space is not available at promised "date in." (Written notice should be provided by lessor if "date in" changes so that lessee can make arrangements for an extension in existing space and to make arrangements with the moving company to change the date of the move.)

16. Side letter indicating special terms such as rent credits (free rent), furniture allowances, build out allowances and other incentives some lessors offer to attract a tenant.
17. Percentage of interest charged for late rent (2% over prime is usually acceptable).
18. Sublease and assignment clauses.
19. Tenant area improvements (workletter):
    a. building standard improvements (e.g., partitions, doors, acoustical ceilings, window and floor coverings, etc.)— quantities specified;
    b. cash allowance;
    c. special construction requirements;
    d. identification of contracting party (tenant or landlord);
    e. use of specific design and/or construction contractors.
20. Integral improvements made by tenant:
    a. claimed by tenant upon vacancy;
    b. reimbursement (fair market value) by landlord upon tenant vacancy.
21. Casualty insurance terms (provided by landlord or tenant):
    a. all-risk coverage, exclusion;
    b. subrogation waiver;
    c. restoration terms after a major loss;
    d. termination of lease.
22. Arbitration of disputes.
23. Special concessions.

Premises and Facilities

1. Location in or near financial district.
2. Location on an appropriate floor.
3. Review need or availability of the following space:
   a. public lobby and facilities, including security;
   b. reception area;
   c. partners' offices;
   d. firm administrator's office;
   e. managers' offices;
   f. tax department;
   g. management services department;
   h. staff rooms;
   i. computer/data entry area;
   j. secretarial/work processing stations;
   k. bookkeeping;
   l. duplicating room;
   m. file room;
   n. supply room;
   o. tax library;

    p. other library;

    q. conference room(s);

    r. coffee room;

    s. women's washroom (in office);

    t. men's washroom (in office);

    u. private washrooms for partners and clients;

    v. shower/exercise facility.

4. Screening work space of receptionist, if required.
5. Location and nature of filing facilities:
    a. number of areas required;
    b. file space required;
    c. limited access for staff and outsiders;
    d. availability of storage space for inactive files;
    e. fireproofing considerations;
    f. floor load capacities.
6. Support for communications and information systems:
    a. communications and electric closets;
    b. floor loadings and structure concerns;
    c. risers and conduit space;
    d. communications facilities available from local telephone company's central office;
    e. rooftop communications facilities;
    f. adequate power distribution;
    g. sufficient heating, ventilating and air-conditioning capabilities.
7. Availability of parking space:
    a. partners;
    b. staff;
    c. clients.
8. Availability, during office off-hours of:
    a. admission to building;
    b. elevators;
    c. utilities, including air-conditioning;
    d. night security guard;
    e. other security features.
9. Listing of firm name(s) and partners' names:
    a. names to be listed (including affiliates);
    b. building directory and exterior signs;
    c. office doors;
    d. lessor specifications as to style, size, etc.;
    e. other identification.

General Furnishing Considerations

1. Carpeting.
2. Blinds or draperies.

3. Style of furniture.
4. Location and space requirements of furniture.
5. Wall coverings.

Summary of Estimated Costs

1. *Initial costs* (does not include leasehold):
    a. prepaid rent or deposits; $ _____
    b. furniture additions;   _____
    c. utility prepayments and telephone set-up costs;   _____
    d. other set-up costs;   _____
    e. broker fees;   _____
    f. legal fees;   _____
    g. moving company fees;   _____
    h. costs for printing new stationery and
        announcements;   _____
    i. construction and architectural costs;   _____
    j. additional insurance costs.   _____

2. *Leasehold cost**
    Required improvements and the estimated cost if not
    furnished by lessor:
    a. partitioning; $ _____
    b. lighting;   _____
    c. floor covering (other than installed);   _____
    d. window covering;   _____
    e. cabinets and shelving;   _____
    f. heat and air conditioning;   _____
    g. initial decorations;   _____
    h. special power supply;   _____
    i. directory listing;   _____
    j. door inscriptions.   _____
        Total initial costs (1 & 2) $ _____

3. *Annual operating costs*:
    a. Rental (lease plus escalation costs); $ _____
    b. Utilities (not paid by lessor);   _____
        • electricity and gas   _____
        • additional for air conditioning
          (including off-hours costs)   _____
        • water   _____
        • telephone   _____

_____

*When determining leasehold costs, also consider:
1. Contributions or allowance, if any, from lessor.
2. Required conformity to lessor's specifications.
3. Use of an interior decorator.

c. Property taxes;   _____

d. Other taxes;   _____

e. Other service costs (including any off-hours costs);
   - office cleaning   _____
   - window cleaning   _____
   - elevator service   _____
   - miscellaneous costs   _____

f. maintenance and repairs;   _____

g. redecoration;   _____

h. fire alarm and sprinkler systems;   _____

i. parking;   _____

j. insurance;   _____

k. security costs;   _____

l. other _____   _____

Total estimated operating costs $_____

Summary of Statistics

1. Rentable area:
   - a. Currently   _____ sq ft.
   - b. Estimated in three years   _____ sq. ft.
2. Personnel required:
   - a. Currently   _____ persons
   - b. Estimated in three years   _____ persons
3. Area per person:
   - a. Currently   _____ sq. ft.
   - b. Estimated in three years   _____ sq. ft.
4. Annual rent per square foot:
   - a. Basic lease $_____ sq. ft.
   - b. Amortization of leasehold $_____ sq. ft.
     - Total rent per square foot $_____ sq. ft.
5. Annual costs:
   - a. Total rent costs (including amortization of leasehold) $_____
   - b. Operating costs $_____

   Total Annual Costs $_____

SOURCE: AICPA, *MAP Handbook,* rev. ed. (New York: AICPA, 1990), 210:31–33.

AICPA Services for Small Firms

Listed below are AICPA member services of particular interest to new CPA firm owners. For more information, write the AICPA, 1211 Avenue of the Americas, New York, N.Y. 10036 or call the numbers listed below.

Services and Publications of the Management of an Accounting Practice Committee

National Practice Management Conferences, targeted toward managing partners of local firms, offer a practical approach to practice management. Geared to mid-size and larger local firms, but open to all. Two each year: summer and fall. (212) 575–3814

National Small Firm Conferences, designed for sole practitioners and firms with two to four partners, provide practical guidance on how to operate a successful, small firm. As with all MAP conferences, exchange of information on management problems and solutions with other practitioners is emphasized. Two conferences annually: summer and fall. (212) 575–3814

National Marketing Conferences are for firms of all sizes but are designed primarily for partners responsible for marketing and Marketing Directors. The conferences cover techniques for successful practice development. One annually in June. (212) 575–3814

MAP Handbook, a comprehensive 1,000 page, three-volume, looseleaf reference service on practice management, is updated annually. It includes more than 200 forms, sample letters, checklists, worksheets, all easy to reproduce or adapt for your practice needs. It provides detailed financial data and policy information for various-sized firms that enable you to evaluate your performance with comparable sized firms. Topics covered include developing an accounting practice, administration, personnel, partnerships, and management data.

For information   (212) 575-3826
To order   1-800-323-8724

MAP Selected Readings, a companion book to the *MAP Handbook,* is a reader's digest of over 500 pages of articles on successful practice management, specially compiled from leading professional journals. The articles contain numerous profit-making ideas for your practice. A new *Selected Readings* edition is published annually.

For information   (212) 575-3826
To order   1-800-323-8724

MAPWORKS—DOCUMAP contains documents from the *MAP Handbook* dealing with organization, client engagements, and personnel on diskette. Available in three formats: APG2—No. 016911, ASCII—No. 090080, and WordPerfect 4.2—No. 090081.

U.S.   1-800-334-6961
New York State 1-800-248-0445
Outside U.S.   (212) 575-7017

Organizational Documents: A Guide for Partnerships and Professional Corporations is a guide to drafting a partnership agreement or corporate documents. Includes a sample partnership agreement with more than 100 provisions and a step-by-step approach to incorporating. Book—No. 012640, WordPerfect 4.2 disk—No. 090091, ASCII disk—No. 090090, book and WordPerfect 4.2 disk set—No. 090096, and ASCII disk and book set—No. 090095.

U.S.   1-800-334-6961
New York State 1-800-248-0445
Outside U.S.   (212) 575-7017

Other MAP Committee publications will be published in the future, including an upcoming guide on practice continuation agreements, a must for sole practitioners and other small firms. Watch AICPA "Update" for announcements of publication dates.

The **MAP Inquiry Service** responds to member inquiries concerning firm management and administration. Need more help? The MAP staff can put you in touch with experienced CPAs or consultants who can assist you with your special problems.   (212) 575-3814

The *MAP Roundtable Discussion Manual* contains guidelines for organizing a MAP roundtable discussion group. Such a group helps firms find practical solutions to common issues or problems through regular meetings and information exchange. The guidelines include sample correspondence, forms to administer a roundtable, and twenty suggested discussion outlines on topical management issues.   (212) 575–3814

Other Technical and Managerial Assistance

The **Technical Information Service (TIS)** responds to members' inquiries about practice problems (except tax and legal questions and those involving litigation).

U.S. (including Puerto Rico and Virgin Islands)   1–800–223–4158
New York State   1–800–522–5430

AICPA **Software Support** assists practitioners in using AICPA Software and maintains a data bank of software programs of interest to CPAs to help members locate a particular software.   (212) 575–5412

The **AICPA Library** researches members' requests for information, provides bibliographies, and loans materials by mail. The library compiles and publishes the *Accountants' Index.* The index is also available as an on-line database, "Accountants," through ORBIT Search Service at (703) 442–0900 or 1–800–456–7248. The library's collection includes all of the books and journals listed in the *Accountants' Index,* the annual reports of 6,500 companies, extensive tax services as well as access to hundreds of on-line databases. A Price Schedule and *Library Guide* are available.

U.S. (including Puerto Rico and Virgin Islands)   1–800–223–4155
New York State   1–800–522–5434

The *Professional Ethics Division* responds to members' questions about the application of the code of professional conduct to specific practice situations. The division also investigates complaints of alleged violations of the code of professional conduct.   (212) 575–3841

The AICPA *Continuing Professional Education (CPE) Division*, the largest developer of CPE programs for CPAs, offers courses in a variety of formats. The CPE Division also offers more than 200 continuing professional education self-study courses in audio, video, text, and computer based formats. All of these courses are convenient CPE options for local practitioners. To plan a CPE program appropriate for your firm, call the CPE Division or your state society.

Toll-free—except New York State   1–800–242–7269
New York State   (212) 575–5696

Through the **National Automated Accounting Research Systems (NAARS)**, local practitioners can research corporate and governmental financial statements, footnotes, and auditors' reports from thousands of annual reports as well as from authoritative literature. NAARS may be accessed through a personal computer or on an individual inquiry basis through the AICPA Information Retrieval Department.

(212) 575–6393

The AICPA's **Total On-line Tax and Accounting Library (TOTAL)** is an AICPA service that allows low-cost access to NAARS, LEXIS® tax libraries and other on-line libraries such as NEXIS® at Mead Data Central.

(212) 575–7075

The **Quality Review Program** is a practice monitoring program established to give emphasis and attention to assuring quality in the performance of accounting and auditing engagements by AICPA members. All AICPA members in public practice are required to participate in a peer review or quality review once every three years. (212) 575–8264

The **Consulting Review Program** offers a firm an opportunity to have its quality control system evaluated by a qualified practitioner on a confidential, risk-free basis. (212) 575–5477

The **Division for CPA Firms**, including a Private Companies Practice Section and an SEC Practice Section, provides a self-regulatory system for member firms and a structure for addressing the special needs of firms serving SEC clients and those serving private companies. A firm may join either section or both. (212) 575–3662

Voluntary dues-paying membership divisions have been established for AICPA members with special interests in taxation, personal financial planning (PFP), and management advisory services (MAS). Benefits of membership in these divisions include publications, practice aids, newsletters, and surveys as well as other activities. Each division also holds national meetings that members are encouraged to attend.

Tax Division (202) 737–6600
PFP (212) 575–3644
MAS (212) 575–6290

Members of MAS can also use **Referral Services for MAS** to request the names of other division members who have experience in any of thirty-six types of MAS and MAS experience in any of twenty-two different industries. (212) 575–6290

The **Management Advisory Services (MAS) Small Business Consulting Practices Subcommittee** develops publications to assist practitioners in identifying and solving problems of smaller enterprises.

(212) 575–6290

National Conferences are held annually on such topics as accounting and auditing, private companies practice, MAS, federal taxation, data processing, estate planning, savings institutions, banking, and firm administration.

(212) 575–6451

Other Publications

Note: Except where listed, call the **Order Department:**

U.S. 1–800–334–6961
New York State 1–800–248–0445
Outside U.S.   (212) 575–7017

Studies and guidelines on subjects of interest to the local practitioners are issued by the Accounting Standards, Auditing Standards, Federal Taxation, and MAS Divisions and by the Accounting Review Services Committee.

The *Audit and Accounting Manual,* available as a looseleaf service and in paperback, is a nonauthoritative kit of practice aids that includes accountants' reports, quality control forms, working papers, confirmation requests, and various checklists. No. 007245.

Accounting and Auditing Update Handbook 1990 is a compact, portable review of new rules issued by FASB and AICPA governing accounting and auditing practice. Emphasis is on techniques and procedures for compliance in actual engagements. No. 029615.

The Accountant's Business Manual contains up-to-date information on a wide range of business services: taxes, insurance, investments, bankruptcy, etc. The manual is published as a single, loose-leaf volume; semiannual supplements are sent automatically. No. 029418.

The Accountant's Business Manual Paperback Series consists of three softbound handbooks on **General Business Information, Business Entities** and **Employment Issues** reprinted from the *Accountant's Business Manual.* Each volume may be ordered separately.

Annual *Tax Practice Guides and Checklists,* available in book and APG2 and WordPerfect 4.2 diskette forms, provides checklists for all principal forms used in preparation and review of Federal tax returns, plus a draft 1040 Engagement Letter and miscellaneous practice guides.

A pamphlet, *Communications With Audit Committees*, assists members in explaining the auditor's responsibilities to communicate to audit committees pertinent information during an audit. No. 022029.

A pamphlet, *The New Auditor's Report—What it Means to You*, assists members in explaining the revised auditor's standard report to clients and others. No. 022014.

A booklet, *Understanding Audits and the Auditor's Report: A Guide for Financial Statement Users*, contains a description of the nature of an audit, illustrative examples of the auditor's standard report, and discussions of the responsibilities of management, the auditor, and users. No. 058514.

Automobile Tax Diary is a vest pocket size log for recording deductible expenses of automobile use in business, medical, and charitable activities. The diaries may be ordered in quantity for distribution to clients, imprinted with firm name, address, and phone number. No. 066012.

A booklet, *The CPA and Management Consulting*, describes the general nature and some specific types of MAS. Designed for distribution to clients and other interested parties, it explains how a company can benefit by using its CPA as a business advisor or as a management consultant. No. 338585.

Subscriptions

For more information, please write the AICPA, P.O. Box 1002, New York, N.Y. 10108–1002.

The *Journal of Accountancy*, a monthly magazine, runs major "nuts and bolts" articles on practice management growth and development. The **"Practitioners' Forum"** column, for example, includes advice from colleagues on aspects of operating a practice, while **"For the Practicing Auditor,"** a bi-monthly column, includes articles on audit practice issues and recent auditing technical developments.

The *Tax Adviser*, a monthly magazine, includes articles about taxation, interpretations, tax-planning pointers, and recent developments.

Practicing CPA, a monthly newsletter, includes short articles on practice management and practical applications of professional standards for local practitioners.

A semimonthly newsletter entitled *CPA Letter* provides members with information about current technical and professional developments.

The *CPA Client Tax Letter* is a quarterly newsletter for practitioners' clients devoted solely to taxes.

The *CPA Client Bulletin*, a monthly client newsletter covering taxes, MAS advice, and personal finance suggestions, is available to practitioners for distribution to their clients.

Digest of Washington Issues is a bimonthly publication describing major issues of importance to the accountancy profession.

Communications

The **Public Relations and Communications Division** coordinates national public relations efforts on behalf of the accounting profession. Through the production of speeches, brochures, and video productions, the division informs the public of the wide range of services available from local practitioners. These materials are available to members to assist them in their communications and marketing efforts. The division also offers advice on press relations, issues newspaper releases, issues radio and television public service announcements, and conducts media training sessions.

Speeches and Brochure	(212) 575-5574
Video Production	(212) 575-3883
CPA Letter	(212) 575-6274
Press Relations	(212) 575-3879

Professional Recognition

The **Examinations Division**, under the direction of the AICPA Board of Examiners, prepares the Uniform CPA Examination and operates the Advisory Grading Services, both are used by all boards of accountancy to license CPAs. The Uniform CPA Examination ensures that CPAs possess a minimum level of technical competence. Also, the Examinations Division, under the direction of the Specialization Accreditation Board, develops and manages the Accredited Specialist Designation Programs and monitors the Accredited Personal Financial Specialist (APFS) Designation Program—the first specialist designation program.

(212) 575-6495

The **Relations with Educators Division** develops recruiting literature and films to keep educators and students informed about the opportunities in public accounting practice and, through its Accounting Testing Program, offers a firm a series of tests for personal evaluation.

(212) 575–6357

The **State Legislation Department** works closely with the state societies on accountancy legislation that protects the interests of all practitioners and the general public.   (202) 737–6600

The **Washington Office** monitors federal legislation and regulations and submits comments on matters affecting small firms.   (202) 737–6600

Member Benefits

The **AICPA Professional Liability Insurance Program** offers coverage for claims arising from alleged negligence in the practice of public accounting.   1–800–221–3023

AICPA Retirement Plans offer firms defined contribution and profit sharing programs (with a variety of investment options) for providing retirement benefits to proprietors and partners, as well as firm members and employees.

Toll-free—except New York State   1–800–223–8075
New York State—call collect   (914) 697–8631

The **Benevolent Fund** helps members, former members, and members' families through periods of financial difficulty.   (212) 575–3659

AICPA Insurance Trust

Life Insurance Programs

The **CPA Plan**, for individual CPAs, provides up to $750,000 of life insurance plus $750,000 of accidental death benefits.

Toll-free—except New York State   1–800–223–7473
New York State—call collect   (212) 973–6200

The **Spouse Life Insurance**, for CPA Plan participants provides the same levels of coverage as offered under the CPA Plan.

Toll-free—except New York State   1–800–221–3021
New York State—call collect   (212) 973–6200

The **Group Insurance Plan**, for public accounting firms, provides up to $200,000 of life insurance plus $200,000 of accidental-death benefits. The plan is available to owners of firms and their employees.

Toll-free—except New York State   1–800–221–3019
New York State—call collect   (212) 973–6200

Disability Insurance Program

The **Long-Term Disability Income Plan**, for individual CPAs, provides up to $5,000 of monthly benefits. The plan includes liberal definitions and covers reasonable and necessary rehabilitation costs.

Toll-free—except New York State   1–800–221–4722
New York State—call collect   (212) 973–6200

Liability Insurance Program

The **Personal Liability Umbrella Security Plan (PLUS Plan)** for members provides up to $5 million coverage for claims for personal liability, bodily injury or property damage which exceed primary automobile and homeowners or renters coverage.

Toll-free—except New York State   1–800–221–3021
New York State—call collect   (212) 973–6200

Annotated Bibliography

Books

AICPA. *Management of an Accounting Practice Handbook.* rev. ed. New York: AICPA 1989. Published by AICPA, New York, New York, and Practitioners Publishing Company, P.O. Box 966, Fort Worth, Texas 76101–0966. To order, call 1–800–323–8724.

This is the most definitive resource available on accounting practice management topics. It is a product of the AICPA's MAP committee. The handbook's contributing authors are all noted authorities in their respective areas. A number are prominent national speakers, and some are current and past members of the AICPA's MAP Committee.

The handbook has five sections: Developing an Accounting Practice, Administration, Personnel, Partnerships, and Management Data. The first two sections are the most pertinent to starting a practice, covering a range of topics from organization and practice growth to billing and collections, review procedures, insurance and legal matters, and malpractice issues.

Personnel and partnership topics will be pertinent to all at a later date, and to some currently. The last section on Management Data contains information on suggested financial statements of accounting firms, information on financial data of over 2,500 accounting firms (The Texas Society's *National Report),* including profitability, billing rates, financial profiles, and hours worked. This section also contains management review questionnaires used by the AICPA's MAP Committee's local Firm Management Review Program and should serve as a valuable self-evaluation aid.

AICPA. *MAP Selected Readings.* rev. ed. New York: AICPA and PPC, 1989. This is also available through Practitioners Publishing Company. To order, call 1–800–323–8724.

Each year, the AICPA's MAP Committee selects over 100 informative and timely articles on MAP-related topics, from professional and business publications. The articles correlate to the table of contents and topics covered in the *MAP Handbook,* for example, chapter 102, ''Starting a Practice.''

The reader has the benefit of reviewing a number of articles on a given topic, knowing experienced practitioners have reviewed various articles and publications in an effort to select the most noteworthy and pertinent dissertations available.

Gallagher, Robert J. *Merging Your CPA Firm: A Guide to Successful Acquisition or Sale of an Accounting Practice.* Colorado Springs, Colorado: Shepard's/McGraw-Hill, Inc., 1988.

This is a timely presentation that deals with a number of critical issues, including premerger considerations, valuing an accounting practice, the human element in mergers, dissolution of a merger, and postmerger matters.

The book offers questionnaires, sample agreements, and checklists, as well as selected reading lists at the end of each chapter.

Although generally directed toward firms larger than the beginning practitioner's, the concepts are essentially the same. Of particular note in Mr. Gallagher's book is his concept of valuing a practice by looking at the quality of earnings of a company, not necessarily the gross earnings.

Goldsmith, Charles. *Selling Skills for CPAs: How to Bring in New Business.* New York: McGraw-Hill Book Company, 1985.

This is a timely dissertation by the coordinator of management development of Deloitte, Haskins & Sells on CPAs and selling. Mr. Goldsmith covers selling professional services, what motivates prospects, making contact, telephone selling, meetings and presentations, answering objections and gaining the thin edge that spells the difference between winning and losing in selling professional services.

Mahon, James J. *The Marketing of Professional Accounting Services.* New York: John Wiley & Sons, 1978.

Written and published before the advent of the revised ethics of the late 1970s, which removed the ban on advertising and solicitation, James Mahon's book offers guidelines to selling and marketing professional services in a more conventional manner. He deals with communications, forums for gaining visibility, and the accountant's services and marketplace. His views and opinions are still pertinent to marketing professional services today.

Olson, Wallace E. *The Accounting Profession, Years of Trial: 1969-1980.* New York: AICPA, 1982.

This overview of what has happened in the profession in the preceding decade offers a view of major problems facing the profession, including litigation against auditors, federal government intervention, accounting standards, ethics and enforcement, and specialization.

Olson's book is particularly significant in that many of the issues identified in the '70s, such as specialization, standards proliferation and changes in ethics are now being addressed.

Rachlin, Norman S. *Eleven Steps to Building a Profitable Accounting Practice.* New York: McGraw-Hill Book Company, 1983.

Rachlin's book explores the initialization process, fees, personnel, marketing, and specialization. He concludes with a long-range plan and a look at the future. His appendixes are particularly useful, containing a considerable number of sample forms.

Stevens, Mark. *The Accounting Wars.* New York: Macmillan Publishing Company, 1985.

Chapter 6 in this book is particularly pertinent to aspiring practitioners. Titled ''Too Big to Be Small, Too Small to Be Big: Competing with the Big Eight,'' it deals with two smaller firms competing in the competitive accounting environment. Again, the beginner needs to scale the issues down to his or her own competitive environment's size, but the situations will be similar.

Williams, Albert S. *Starting Your Own CPA Firm.* Denver: Colorado Society of Certified Public Accountants, 1988.

A one-day CPE course that is currently offered fifteen to eighteen times each year throughout the nation, *Starting Your Own CPA Firm,* deals with many of the topics noted in this dissertation, including financing, obtaining clientele, rate setting, billing and collecting, and difficult clients.

The author has accumulated significant survey data from these sessions that helped to formulate much of the underlying data in the material.

Periodicals

Besides the foregoing publications, initial practitioners should have access to three periodicals of particular note. A number of issues of these publications will be represented in the *MAP Selected Readings* previously cited.

- *Journal of Accountancy,* particularly the "Practitioners Forum" department. AICPA, 1211 Avenue of the Americas, New York, New York 10036–8775.

- *The Practicing CPA,* an AICPA publication designed for the local practitioner. AICPA, 1211 Avenue of the Americas, New York, New York 10036–8775.

- *The Practical Accountant,* a periodical dealing with accounting and taxes in everyday practice. Warren, Gorham & Lamont, Inc., 210 South Street, Boston, Massachusetts 02111.

About the Author

Albert S. Williams began practicing public accounting in 1966. Since then he has worked at a national accounting firm, regional and local firms, and as a sole practitioner in a broad range of accounting fields. He has applied his expertise in business valuations, acquisitions and dispositions, management consulting, business plan development, budgeting, auditing, and tax return preparation for a diverse range of clients, including other CPAs. He has served as a technical advisor to the Colorado State Board of Accountancy and investigated and testified in cases where CPA practices had floundered because of problems associated with standards and ethics. He now restricts his practice to management consulting and litigation support.

Mr. Williams has written numerous articles for national publications and is the author of several continuing education courses for the Colorado Society of CPAs. He has been an adjunct professor for local colleges and has lectured and taught nationwide on practice management topics and staff training for various state CPA societies as well as for the AICPA. He is the author of the Colorado CPA Society's course on ''Starting Your Own CPA Firm'' and has taught the course to approximately 3,000 prospective owners in the past fourteen years.

Mr. Williams is a former chairman of the Colorado Society's Management of an Accounting Practice committee, and a former member of both the Colorado Society's board of directors and Professional Ethics board. Previously, he was a member of the AICPA's Management of an Accounting Practice committee and is currently active in the Colorado Society. He holds a B.S. in Business Administration from Arizona State University.